ALSO BY DAVE BARRY

# Dave Barry's Complete Guide to Guys

# Dave Barry's Complete Guide to Guys

## A FAIRLY SHORT BOOK

# Dave Barry

Random House    New York

*This book is dedicated to whoever
invented the remote control.
(I'd look up this person's name,
but I don't feel like getting off the sofa.)*

# Contents

# Introduction

## Guys vs. Men

THIS IS A BOOK about guys. It's *not* a book about men. There are already way too many books about men, and most of them are *way* too serious.

*Men* itself is a serious word, not to mention *manhood* and *manly*. Such words make being male sound like a very important activity, as opposed to what it primarily consists of, namely, possessing a set of minor and frequently unreliable organs.

But men tend to attach great significance to Manhood. This results in certain characteristically masculine, by which I mean stupid, behavioral patterns that can produce unfortunate results such as violent crime, war, spitting, and ice hockey. These things have given males a bad name.[1] And the "Men's Movement," which is supposed to bring out the more positive aspects of Manliness, seems to be densely populated with loons and goobers.

So I'm saying that there's another way to look at males: not as aggressive macho dominators; not as sensitive, liberated, hugging drummers; but as *guys.*

And what, exactly, do I mean by "guys"? I don't know. I haven't thought that much about it. One of the major characteristics of guyhood is that we guys don't spend a lot of time pondering our deep innermost feelings. There is a serious question in my mind about whether guys actually *have* deep innermost feelings, unless you count, for example, loyalty to the Detroit Tigers, or fear of bridal showers.

But although I can't define exactly what it means to be a guy, I can describe certain guy characteristics, such as:

## Guys Like Neat Stuff

By "neat," I mean "mechanical and unnecessarily complex." I'll give you an example. Right now I'm typ-

---

[1]Specifically, "asshole."

ing these words on an *extremely* powerful computer. It's the latest in a line of maybe ten computers I've owned, each one more powerful than the last. My computer is chock full of RAM and ROM and bytes and megahertzes and various other items that enable a computer to kick data-processing butt. It is probably capable of supervising the entire U.S. air-defense apparatus while simultaneously processing the tax return of every resident of Ohio. I use it mainly to write a newspaper column. This is an activity wherein I sit and stare at the screen for maybe ten minutes, then, using only my forefingers, slowly type something like:

*Henry Kissinger looks like a big wart.*

I stare at this for another ten minutes, have an inspiration, then amplify the original thought as follows:

*Henry Kissinger looks like a big fat wart.*

Then I stare at that for another ten minutes, pondering whether I should try to work in the concept of "hairy."

This is absurdly simple work for my computer. It sits there, humming impatiently, bored to death, passing the time between keystrokes via brain-teaser activities such as developing a Unified Field Theory of the universe and translating the complete works of Shakespeare into rap.[2]

---

[2]To be or not? I got to *know.*
Might kill myself by the end of the *show.*

In other words, this computer is absurdly overqualified to work for me, and yet soon, I guarantee, I will buy an *even more powerful* one. I won't be able to stop myself. I'm a guy.

Probably the ultimate example of the fundamental guy drive to have neat stuff is the Space Shuttle. Granted, the guys in charge of this program *claim* it has a Higher Scientific Purpose, namely to see how humans function in space. But of course we have known for years how humans function in space: They float around and say things like: "Looks real good, Houston!"

No, the real reason for the existence of the Space Shuttle is that it is one humongous and spectacularly gizmo-intensive item of hardware. Guys can tinker with it practically forever, and occasionally even get it to work, and use it to place *other* complex mechanical items into orbit, where they almost immediately break, which provides a great excuse to send the Space Shuttle up *again.* It's Guy Heaven.

Other results of the guy need to have stuff are Star Wars, the recreational boating industry, monorails, nuclear weapons, and wristwatches that indicate the phase of the moon. I am not saying that women haven't been involved in the development or use of this stuff. I'm saying that, without guys, this stuff probably would not exist; just as, without women, virtually every piece of

furniture in the world would still be in its original posi-
tion. Guys do not have a basic need to rearrange furniture. Whereas a woman who could cheerfully use the
same computer for fifty-three years will rearrange her
furniture on almost a weekly basis, sometimes in the
dead of night. She'll be sound asleep in bed, and suddenly, at 2 A.M., she'll be awakened by the urgent
thought: *The blue-green sofa needs to go perpendicular to
the wall instead of parallel, and it needs to go there RIGHT
NOW.* So she'll get up and move it, which of course
necessitates moving other furniture, and soon she has
rearranged her entire living room, shifting great big
heavy pieces that ordinarily would require several
burly men to lift, because there are few forces in Nature
more powerful than a woman who needs to rearrange
furniture. Every so often a guy will wake up to discover
that, because of his wife's overnight efforts, he now lives
in an entirely different house.

(I realize that I'm making gender-based generalizations here, but my feeling is that if God did not want us
to make gender-based generalizations, She would not
have given us genders.)

## Guys Like a Really Pointless Challenge

Not long ago I was sitting in my office at the *Miami
Herald*'s Sunday magazine, *Tropic*, reading my fan

mail,[3] when I heard several of my guy coworkers in the hallway talking about how fast they could run the forty-yard dash. These are guys in their thirties and forties who work in journalism, where the most demanding physical requirement is the ability to digest vending-machine food. In other words, these guys have absolutely no need to run the forty-yard dash.

But one of them, Mike Wilson, was writing a story about a star high-school football player who could run it in 4.38 seconds. Now if Mike had written a story about, say, a star high-school poet, none of my guy coworkers would have suddenly decided to find out how well they could write sonnets. But when Mike turned in his story, they became *deeply* concerned about how fast they could run the forty-yard dash. They were so concerned that the magazine editor, Tom Shroder, decided that they should get a stopwatch and go out to a nearby park and find out. Which they did, a bunch of guys taking off their shoes and running around barefoot in a public park on company time.

This is what I heard them talking about, out in the hall. I heard Tom, who was thirty-eight years old, saying that his time in the forty had been 5.75 seconds. And I thought to myself: This is ridiculous. These are middle-aged guys, supposedly adults, and they're out

[3]Typical fan letter: "Who cuts your hair? Beavers?"

there *bragging* about their performance in this stupid juvenile footrace. Finally I couldn't stand it anymore.

"Hey!" I shouted. "*I could beat 5.75 seconds.*"

So we went out to the park and measured off forty yards, and the guys told me that I had three chances to make my best time. On the first try my time was 5.78 seconds, just three-hundredths of a second slower than Tom's, even though, at forty-five, I was seven years older than he. So I just *knew* I'd beat him on the second attempt if I ran really, really hard, which I did for a solid ten yards, at which point my left hamstring muscle, which had not yet shifted into Spring Mode from Mail-Reading Mode, went, and I quote, "pop."

I had to be helped off the field. I was in considerable pain, and I was obviously not going to be able to walk right for weeks. The other guys were very sympathetic, especially Tom, who took the time to call me at home, where I was sitting with an ice pack on my leg and twenty-three Advil in my bloodstream, so he could express his concern.

"Just remember," he said, *"you didn't beat my time."*

There are countless other examples of guys rising to meet pointless challenges. Virtually all sports fall into this category, as well as a large part of U.S. foreign policy. ("I'll bet you can't capture Manuel Noriega!" "Oh YEAH??")

## Guys Do Not Have a Rigid and Well-Defined Moral Code

This is not the same as saying that guys are bad. Guys *are* capable of doing bad things, but this generally happens when they try to be Men and start becoming manly and aggressive and stupid. When they're being just plain guys, they aren't so much actively *evil* as they are *lost*. Because guys have never really grasped the Basic Human Moral Code, which I believe was invented by women millions of years ago when all the guys were out engaging in some other activity, such as seeing who could burp the loudest. When they came back, there were certain rules that they were expected to follow unless they wanted to get into Big Trouble, and they have been trying to follow these rules ever since, with extremely irregular results. Because guys have never *internalized* these rules. Guys are similar to my small auxiliary backup dog, Zippy, a guy dog[4] who has been told numerous times that he is *not* supposed to (1) get into the kitchen garbage or (2) poop on the floor. He knows that these are the rules, but he has never really understood *why,* and sometimes he gets to thinking: Sure, I am *ordinarily* not supposed to get into the garbage, but obviously this rule is not meant to apply when there are certain ex-

[4] I also have a female dog, Earnest, who *never* breaks the rules.

tenuating[5] circumstances, such as (1) somebody just threw away some perfectly good seven-week-old Kung Pao Chicken, and (2) I am home alone.

And so when the humans come home, the kitchen floor has been transformed into GarbageFest USA, and Zippy, who usually comes rushing up, is off in a corner disguised in a wig and sunglasses, hoping to get into the Federal Bad Dog Relocation Program before the humans discover the scene of the crime.

When I yell at him, he frequently becomes so upset that he poops on the floor.

Morally, most guys are just like Zippy, only taller and usually less hairy. Guys are *aware* of the rules of moral behavior, but they have trouble keeping these rules in the forefronts of their minds at certain times, especially the present. This is especially true in the area of faithfulness to one's mate. I realize, of course, that there are countless examples of guys being faithful to their mates until they die, usually as a result of being eaten by their mates immediately following copulation. Guys outside of the spider community, however, do not have a terrific record of faithfulness.

I'm not saying guys are scum. I'm saying that many guys who consider themselves to be committed to their

---

[5]I am taking some liberties here with Zippy's vocabulary. More likely, in his mind, he uses the term *mitigating*.

marriages will stray if they are confronted with over-whelming temptation, defined as "virtually any temp-tation."

Okay, so maybe I *am* saying guys are scum. But they're not *mean-spirited* scum. And few of them—even when they are out of town on business trips, far from their wives, and have a clear-cut opportunity—will poop on the floor.

## Guys Are Not Great at Communicating Their Intimate Feelings, Assuming They Have Any

This is an aspect of guyhood that is very frustrating to women. A guy will be reading the newspaper, and the phone will ring; he'll answer it, listen for ten minutes, hang up, and resume reading. Finally his wife will say: "Who was that?"

And he'll say: "Phil Wonkerman's mom."

(Phil is an old friend they haven't heard from in seventeen years.)

And the wife will say, "Well?"

And the guy will say, "Well what?"

And the wife will say, "What did she *say*?"

And the guy will say, "She said Phil is fine," making it clear by his tone of voice that, although he does not wish to be rude, he is trying to read the newspaper, and he happens to be right in the middle of an important panel of "Calvin and Hobbes."

But the wife, ignoring this, will say, "That's *all* she said?"

And she will not let up. She will continue to ask district-attorney-style questions, forcing the guy to recount the conversation until she's satisfied that she has the entire story, which is that Phil just got out of prison after serving a sentence for a murder he committed when he became a drug addict because of the guilt he felt when his wife died in a freak submarine accident while Phil was having an affair with a nun, but now he's all straightened out and has a good job as a trapeze artist and is almost through with the surgical part of his sex change and recently became happily engaged to marry a prominent member of the Grateful Dead, so in other words he is fine, which is *exactly* what the guy told her in the first place, but is that enough? No. She wants to hear *every single detail.*

Or let's say two couples get together after a long separation. The two women will have a conversation, lasting several days, during which they discuss virtually every significant event that has occurred in their lives and the lives of those they care about, sharing their innermost thoughts, analyzing and probing, inevitably coming to a deeper understanding of each other, and a strengthening of a cherished friendship. Whereas the guys will watch the play-offs.

This is not to say the guys won't share their feelings. Sometimes they'll get quite emotional.

"That's not a FOUL??" they'll say.

Or: "YOU'RE TELLING ME THAT'S NOT A *FOUL???*"

I have a good friend, Gene, and one time, when he was going through a major medical development in his life, we spent a weekend together. During this time Gene and I talked a lot and enjoyed each other's company immensely, but—this is true—the most intimate personal statement he made to me is that he has reached Level 24 of a video game called "Arkanoid." He had even seen the Evil Presence, although he refused to tell me what it looks like. We're very close, but there is a limit.

You may think that my friends and I are Neanderthals, and that a lot of guys are different. This is true. A lot of guys don't use words at *all.* They communicate entirely by nonverbal methods, such as sharing bait.

Are you starting to see what I mean by "guyness"? I'm basically talking about the part of the male psyche that is less serious and/or aggressive than the Manly Manhood part, but still essentially very male. My feeling is that the world would be a much better[6] place if more males would stop trying so hard to be Men and instead settle for being Guys. Think of the historical problems that could have been avoided if more males

---

[6]As measured by total sales of this book.

had been able to keep their genderhood in its proper perspective, both in themselves and in others. ("Hey, Adolf, just because you happen to possess a set of minor and frequently unreliable organs, that is no reason to invade Poland.") And think how much happier women would be if, instead of endlessly fretting about what the males in their lives are thinking, they could relax, secure in the knowledge that the correct answer is: *very little.*

Yes, what we need, on the part of both genders, is more understanding of guyness. And that is why I wrote this book. I intend to explore in detail every major facet of guyhood, including the historical facet, the sociological facet, the physiological facet, the psychosexual facet, and the facet of how come guys spit so much. Every statement of fact you will read in this book is either based on actual laboratory tests, or else I made it up. But you can trust me. I'm a guy.

## Example Chart

| Men | Guys |
|---|---|
| Vince Lombardi | Joe Namath |
| Oliver North | Gilligan |
| Hemingway | Gary Larson |
| Columbus | Whichever astronaut hit the first golf ball on the Moon |
| Superman | Bart Simpson |
| Doberman pinschers | Labrador retrievers |
| Abbott | Costello |
| Captain Ahab | Captain Kangaroo |
| Satan | Snidely Whiplash |
| The pope | Willard Scott |
| Germany | Italy |
| Geraldo | Katie Couric |

## Stimulus-Response Comparison Chart:
## Women vs. Men vs. Guys

| Stimulus | Typical *Woman* Response | Typical *Man* Response | Typical *Guy* Response |
|---|---|---|---|
| An untamed river in the wilderness. | Contemplate its beauty. | Build a dam. | See who can pee the farthest off the dam. |
| A child who is sent home from school for being disruptive in class. | Talk to the child in an effort to determine the cause. | Threaten to send the child to a military academy. | Teach the child how to make armpit farts. |
| Human mortality | Religious faith | The pyramids | Bungee-jumping |

# Dave Barry's
# Complete
# Guide to Guys

# Are You a Guy?

Take This Scientific Quiz
to Determine
Your Guyness Quotient

1. Alien beings from a highly advanced society visit
   the Earth, and you are the first human they en-
   counter. As a token of intergalactic friendship, they
   present you with a small but incredibly sophisticated device that is capable of curing all disease,
   providing an infinite supply of clean energy, wiping
   out hunger and poverty, and permanently eliminat-
   ing oppression and violence all over the entire
   Earth. You decide to:
   a. Present it to the president of the United States.

  b. Present it to the secretary general of the United Nations.

  c. Take it apart.

2. As you grow older, what lost quality of your youthful life do you miss the most?

  a. Innocence.

  b. Idealism.

  c. Cherry bombs.

3. When is it okay to kiss another male?

  a. When you wish to display simple and pure affection without regard for narrow-minded social conventions.

  b. When he is the pope. (*Not* on the lips.)

  c. When he is your brother and you are Al Pacino and this is the only really sportsmanlike way to let him know that, for business reasons, you have to have him killed.

4. What about *hugging* another male?

  a. If he's your father and at least one of you has a fatal disease.

  b. If you're performing the Heimlich maneuver. (And even in this case, you should repeatedly shout: "I am just dislodging food trapped in this male's trachea! I am not in any way aroused!")

  c. If you're a professional baseball player and a teammate hits a home run to win the World Series, you may hug him provided that (1) He is legally within the basepath, (2) Both of you are wearing protective cups, and (3) You also pound him fraternally with your fist hard enough to cause fractures.

5. *Complete this sentence:* A funeral is a good time to
   a. . . . remember the deceased and console his loved ones.
   b. . . . reflect upon the fleeting transience of earthly life.
   c. . . . tell the joke about the guy who has Alzheimer's disease *and* cancer.

6. In your opinion, the ideal pet is:
   a. A cat.
   b. A dog.
   c. A dog that eats cats.

7. You have been seeing a woman for several years. She's attractive and intelligent, and you always enjoy being with her. One leisurely Sunday afternoon the two of you are taking it easy—you're watching a football game; she's reading the papers—when she suddenly, out of the clear blue sky, tells you that she thinks she really loves you, but she can no longer bear the uncertainty of not knowing where your relationship is going. She says she's not asking whether you want to get married; only

whether you believe that you have some kind of future together. What do you say?

a. That you sincerely believe the two of you do have a future, but you don't want to rush it.

b. That although you also have strong feelings for her, you cannot honestly say that you'll be ready anytime soon to make a lasting commitment, and you don't want to hurt her by holding out false hope.

c. That you cannot *believe* the Jets called a draw play on third and seventeen.

8. Okay, so you have decided that you truly love a woman and you want to spend the rest of your life with her—sharing the joys and the sorrows, the triumphs and the tragedies, and all the adventures and opportunities that the world has to offer, come what may. How do you tell her?

a. You take her to a nice restaurant and tell her after dinner.

b. You take her for a walk on a moonlit beach, and you say her name, and when she turns to you, with the sea breeze blowing her hair and the stars in her eyes, you tell her.

c. Tell her *what?*

9. One weekday morning your wife wakes up feeling ill and asks you to get your three children ready for school. Your first question to her is:

a. "Do they need to eat or anything?"
b. "They're in *school* already?"
c. "There are *three* of them?"

10. When is it okay to throw away a set of veteran underwear?

   a. When it has turned the color of a dead whale and developed new holes so large that you're not sure which ones were originally intended for your legs.
   b. When it is down to eight loosely connected underwear molecules and has to be handled with tweezers.
   c. It is *never* okay to throw away veteran underwear. A real guy checks the garbage regularly in case somebody—and we are not naming names, but this would be his wife—is quietly trying to discard his underwear, which she is frankly jealous of, because the guy seems to have a more intimate relationship with it than with her.

11. What, in your opinion, is the *most reasonable* explanation for the fact that Moses led the Israelites all over the place for forty years before they finally got to the Promised Land?

   a. He was being tested.
   b. He wanted them to really appreciate the Promised Land when they finally got there.
   c. He refused to ask directions.

12. What is the human race's single greatest achievement?
   a. Democracy.
   b. Religion.
   c. Remote control.

**How to Score:** Give yourself one point for every time you picked answer "c." A real guy would score at least 10 on this test. In fact, a *real* guy would score at least 15, because he would get the special five-point bonus for knowing the joke about the guy who has Alzheimer's disease *and* cancer.

# 1

# The Role of Guys in History

Men Went to the Moon,
but Guys Invented Mooning

GUYS HAVE PLAYED an important role in history,
but this role has not been given the attention it deserves, because nobody wrote it down. Guys are not
conscientious about writing. Take thank-you notes.
When a couple gets married, the bride very quickly—
sometimes right after her new husband passes out in
their honeymoon-suite hot tub—starts composing per-
sonalized notes thanking their wedding guests for all
the lovely gifts (". . . I didn't know they even *made* a
traveling case for the Salad Shooter").

The bride will keep this up until she has written every single guest; if it was a really big wedding, she may still be thanking people after her divorce ("Aunt Esther, the meat fork is *beautiful,* and I expect to get many happy years of use from it once the surgeons extract it from Roger").

Very few guys write thank-you notes, or any other kind of note. Guys would probably commit a lot more kidnappings if they weren't required to write ransom notes.

My point is that, because guys don't write things down, they are not well represented in the history books. You'll find countless references to *men,* however, because men like to record every detail of their lives, for posterity. Alexander the Great, for example, kept a diary, so that today we can read, in his own handwriting, exactly what he was doing on any given day, as is shown by these actual excerpts:

*327 B.C., Nov. 4—Cloudy today. Conquered Asia Minor.*
*324 B.C., Jan. 6—Note: Find out what "B.C." stands for.*
*323 B.C., May 17—Died at an early age.*

But what about the average guy in Alexander the Great's army? What about *his* contributions to history? Yes, it is important that Alexander extended the influence of such legendary Greek philosophers as Aristotle throughout most of the civilized world, thus significantly affecting the development of Western thought and culture to this very day; but is it not also important that, at the same time, some of his lowly foot soldiers were perfecting the Rubber Spear Trick, or determining that the letters in "Aristotle" can be rearranged to spell "A Tit Loser"?[1]

That is the kind of historical guy accomplishment I'm going to explore in this chapter, starting with a discussion of:

## Prehistoric Guys

Prehistory was a very difficult time for humans. Hostile, vicious, person-eating predators roamed the Earth. Disease was rampant. Mortality rates were horrific. The automatic bank teller was still only a dream.

Back then the clan was the basic unit[2] of society, with the roles of males and females clearly defined. The females cared for the young and gathered roots, which they would soak in water, then peel, then painstakingly pound for hours between two heavy rocks, and finally throw away. "We may be primitive, but we're not stupid enough to eat roots," was their feeling.

Thus the basic food-gathering responsibility fell on the shoulders of the males, who would go off for days at

[1] Also "Tater Silo."
[2] 10 clans = one tribe.

a time to hunt the mighty dinosaur. This was hard work. They had to dig an enormous deep hole, then disguise it by covering it with frail branches,[3] then hide in the bushes, waiting for a mighty dinosaur to come along and fall into the trap. The hunters often waited for long periods, because, unbeknownst to them, dinosaurs had become extinct several million years earlier.

So the males sat around a lot. Some of them eventually became fidgety and went on to develop agriculture, invent primitive tools,[4] etc. But some males—these were the original guys—really *liked* sitting around. Eventually they stopped bothering to dig the hole. They'd just go out into the woods and sit.

"It's not easy, trying to catch dinosaurs," they would tell people, especially their wives. "But if we don't do it, who will?"

They never helped with the roots.

Sitting around for no reason under the guise of being engaged in productive work was the first real guy contribution to human civilization, forming the underlying basis for many modern institutions and activities such as fishing, sales conferences, highway repair, the federal government, and "Customer Service."

This is not to say that prehistoric guys did nothing but sit around. They also invented an activity that has

---

[3]Sometimes they would also use a false beard.
[4]Such as the stone Weed Whacker.

become one of the most dominant forms of guy behavior, now accounting for an estimated 178 *trillion* guy-hours per year in the United States alone.[5] The activity I am referring to, of course, is guys scratching their personal regions. And when I say "scratching," I am not talking about a couple of quick, discreet swipes with the fingernails to relieve a momentary itch. I'm talking about an activity that guys spend way more time and energy on than they do on, for example, home maintenance.

Walk around any populated area and you'll see dozens, maybe hundreds, of guys engaged in scratching themselves. Some will try to be subtle, but usually once they get going they completely lose track of where they are. Before long they're rooting around in their pants using both hands, garden implements, etc., totally oblivious to the world around them. This can lead to trouble.

FIRST MATE ON THE *TITANIC*: Sir, don't you think we should *do* something about it? Maybe change direction? Sir? Sir?

CAPTAIN: *(. . . scratchscratchscratchscratchscratch-scratch . . .)*

One time in the 1970s I was watching a Philadelphia Phillies game on television, and at a key moment the Phillies' manager, Danny Ozark (who looked ex-

---

[5]Source: Phyllis Schlafly.

actly like a guy named "Danny Ozark") walked to the pitcher's mound for a conference. Danny had his back to the camera, and his right hand, seemingly acting on its own, sort of moseyed around to his rear-end region and started exploring, really *probing*, looking as though maybe Danny had lost some vital documents in there. The hand became so energetic that finally even the TV announcers had to start laughing. This was a guy in the middle of a baseball stadium *and* on TV, with the game at a critical juncture, and *still* his number-one priority was scratching himself. He was a guy's guy, that Danny Ozark.

It was also during these primitive times of sitting around with absolutely nothing to do for weeks on end that guys developed golf. There is evidence that guys were playing golf as early as 2 million B.C., using balls made of animal hide and crude clubs fashioned from tree limbs. Amazingly, these early golfers had already invented such fundamental elements of the game as chipping, putting, sand traps, "bogeys," ugly pants, and cheating. There was one element they had not thought of yet, however: holes. The result was that the primitive game lacked focus and tended to meander. Archaeologists now believe that the first humans to cross the land bridge from Asia to North America were a threesome[6] of early guy golfers. ("How many strokes

---

[6]"Four" had not been invented yet.

do you have?" "Okay, I hit two coming down off the glacier, and one from that mastodon there, so this would be, let's see . . . seventeen million." "LIAR!")

## Ancient Egyptian Guys

The most significant achievement of ancient Egyptian guys occurred at the funeral of the great Pharaoh Amentooten III, when some guys invented the famous "Substitute Mummy Filled with Live Weasels" prank. This led to the collapse of the Egyptian empire, but everybody involved agreed it was worth it.

## Guys of Ancient Greece

Greece, in its Golden Age, was the fertile cultural ground from which sprang some of ancient humanity's most glorious contributions to politics, science, and the arts. Guys had nothing to do with this. The major guy contribution involved the ancient Olympics. These were quite different from the games we see today. For one thing, the athletes competed naked,[7] which meant that not only did their Nike logos have to be tattooed directly onto their skin, but also they sometimes found themselves having embarrassing bodily reactions. ("Is that a javelin you're carrying, or are you just glad to see me?")

[7] Ironically, they *showered* with their clothes on.

Also the early Olympic events were extremely grueling, especially the marathon. The first marathon runner ever was a messenger, who was sent from the scene of a great Greek military victory to carry the news to the city of Athens, twenty-six miles away. He ran and ran and ran, and when he finally got to Athens he ran up to the king, gasped out his message,[8] collapsed to the ground, and died.

For a moment the stunned crowd looked down silently at the body of this courageous man. And then one guy, way in the back of the crowd, deeply moved by what he had seen, could no longer remain silent.

"Boo," he said.[9]

And a couple of other guys, hearing this, thought it sounded pretty good, so they joined in.

"Yeah," they said. "Boo."

This was indeed a historic moment, because these guys were *history's first sports fans.* They had made the breakthrough discovery that you could be involved in sports without having to actually *do* anything. Even if you were a totally nonathletic tub of ancient Greek lard who sat around all day eating ancient Greek junk food and couldn't run twenty-six *feet* without falling over and setting off shock waves powerful enough to create several new ancient Greek ruins, you could still pre-

---

[8]His message was "Σδλκσδφσ δσ϶φλω ερϖ νββ☹⚓" (Literally, "My feet are killing me.")

[9]Pronounced "βoo."

tend that you had something to do with a sporting event by shouting uselessly and often unintelligibly at genuine competitors.

In addition to "Boo," ancient Greek guys developed a number of phrases for fans to yell, expressing both criticism ("You suck!") and encouragement ("You suck!"). Within a few centuries, ancient Roman guys were developing advanced fan phraseology that could be used at a wide range of sporting events. ("Hey LION! You call THAT mauling a Christian? My GRAND-MOTHER could maul a Christian better than that!")

## Guys in the Middle Ages

The Middle Ages saw the breakdown of civilization in Western Europe—a severe decline in cultural values and standards; a rapid descent into chaos and near-barbarism. So it was a pretty good time for guys. They could spit pretty much whenever they wanted, and for entertainment, they could go to jousting tournaments and cheer for their favorite knights. ("Hey LANCELOT! You SUCK!")

Still, it wasn't perfect. Most of the available jobs were in agriculture, which was hard work. People would be out in the fields from dawn to dusk, working the dirt with crude farming implements, sweating and toiling day after day, year after year, yet obtaining only mea-ger results.

"Maybe we should plant some seeds or something," they would sometimes remark.

Medieval guys did not care for agriculture. They were always looking for some new lifestyle option, and finally, one day, one of them had a brilliant idea.

"That's *it!*" he said, smacking himself in the forehead. Unfortunately he was holding a crude farming implement at the time, so he fell to the ground, unconscious. But when he woke up, he explained his plan to the other guys, who loved it, and they immediately put it into effect. That night, at dinner, they turned to their wives, and, with anguish in their voices, said: "You know *what?* The Turks got the Holy Land!"

"No!" said the wives, who, in fact, had no idea what the Holy Land was. But the husbands seemed deeply concerned about it, and the early wives didn't want to appear unsympathetic.

"Yes," said the husbands. "I guess this means I'll have to go on a Crusade."

"A what?" asked the wives.

"Don't wait up for me," said the husbands.

And thus was born one of the greatest guy inventions of all time: business travel. Soon thousands of guys were going on Crusades. After several years they'd return home, and they'd hang around a while, listening to their wives complain about the fact that the soil needed tilling and the roof needed thatching and the kids were coming down with the darned plague again. After a couple of weeks, the guys would announce, looking really upset about it, that those lousy Turks *still* had the Holy Land, and off they'd go again.

Meanwhile, guys in Turkey were leaving *their* homes, telling *their* wives that they had to go get the Western Europeans out of Norway. These groups of opposing crusaders generally spent most of their time hanging out in Italy, where, fortunately for them, the Italian restaurant had just been invented. This in turn led to the development of the expense report, which was the forerunner to modern literary fiction.

## Renaissance Guys

The Renaissance saw the rebirth of interest in philosophy, science, and the arts, and above all the rise of humanism—a philosophy centered on the distinctive needs, interests, and ideals of . . . not deities, but *people.* Guys were in favor of this because it resulted in statues of naked women.

There was also a resurgence in theater, with the appearance of such playwrights as the immortal William Shakespeare, whose brilliant comedies and tragedies were extremely popular with guys. ("Hey HAMLET! You SUCK!")

## The Role of Guys in the Protestant Reformation and the Subsequent Political Realignment of Europe

Guys were fishing when this happened.

## Guys and the Age of Exploration

The Age of Exploration began in the fifteenth century when an Italian guy, who historians believe was named Nick, had a couple of glasses of wine, rented a gondola, and attempted to take his wife on a tour of the canals of Venice. He paddled around for a couple of hours, until his wife, noticing that they were in an unfamiliar neighborhood and suspecting that Nick was lost, suggested that he ask somebody for directions. Naturally he would not do this. It is a well-documented fact that guys will not ask for directions. This is a biological thing. This is why it takes several million guy sperm cells, each one wriggling in its own direction, totally confident it knows where it is going, to locate a female egg, despite the fact that the egg is, relative to them, the size of Wisconsin.

So anyway, Nick was paddling and paddling, and night was falling, and his wife was becoming more and more insistent that they should ask somebody where they were, and he was becoming more and more snappish when he told her he knew *exactly* where they were, and finally they both got so angry that they stopped talking altogether, her sitting with her arms folded, him paddling, until they arrived at the North American continent.

"Oh *sure*," said Nick's wife, because when she was *really* angry she spoke English. "You know *exactly* where we are."

"I *do*," said Nick. "This is a shortcut."

On the way back he almost smashed head-on into Christopher Columbus, going the other way.

## Colonial Guys

It was some colonial guys who came up with the idea of dressing up as Indians and throwing a whole lot of tea into Boston Harbor to express the public outrage over the high-handed antidemocratic actions of the British government. Also they had always wanted to try it.

This courageous effort led to the Revolutionary War, during which these same guys engaged in numerous other paramilitary actions, including: dressing up as cowboys and throwing chairs into Boston Harbor, dressing up as French milkmaids and throwing a cow into Boston Harbor, and dressing up as a bunch of ale-consuming guys and throwing up into Boston Harbor. Gen. George Washington showed his awareness of the efforts of these guys when he personally issued a decree stating that they would not be allowed to be in the army "even if everybody else is dead."

## Guys in the Industrial Revolution

The Industrial Revolution saw the world's economic landscape radically transformed by technological breakthroughs in mechanization, steam power, and mass production, thereby permitting the emergence of capitalistic free markets, the creation of vast wealth, and the rise of the middle class as the dominant social element in an urban-industrial society. During this era guys invented the office betting pool.

---

### GUY SCIENCE MILESTONE

On October 8, 1857—decades before Thomas Edison began experimenting with various designs for an incandescent electric light—Alfred A. "Gus" Loogerhalter, working in a small makeshift laboratory in his home, connected the leads from a crude lead-acid battery to the ends of a filament that he had inserted into a sealed glass globe from which he had pumped out all the oxygen. Nothing happened, so he invented the whoopee cushion.

---

## Guys in the Modern Era

As humanity entered the modern era, guys continued to make contributions. Here is just a partial list of the modern benefits that society would probably not enjoy today if it weren't for guys:

1. Mooning
2. Pez

It may seem as though there is nothing more that guys could possibly accomplish, but they continue to make amazing strides forward right up to the present day. I have here a newspaper article from the La Crosse, Wisconsin, *Tribune,* sent in by an alert reader named Sherryl Gingrich[10] concerning three guys—Trygve Thompson, Richard Stakston, and Dan Ellefson—from the town of Westby, Wisconsin. These guys, all in their forties, had a few beers one winter's night and decided it would be a good idea to hurl themselves off a thirty-meter ski jump.

*In a canoe.*

I am not making this up. According to the article, written by Jeff Brown, the guys had talked about canoe-jumping for several years, and this particular night they just decided to do it. So they hauled a sixteen-foot canoe up to the top, got in—the article says that Ellefson, sitting in the back, had an *oar*[11]—and pushed off. The canoe flew down the jump, rocketed off into space, and—you guessed it—smashed head-on into Christopher Columbus.

No, seriously, the canoe landed at the bottom travel-

[10]Sherryl will receive, as a token of my appreciation, this handsome foot-note mention.

[11]"He was going to steer," Stakston is quoted as saying.

ing at approximately fourteen thousand miles per hour and flipped over. Miraculously, the three occupants suffered only cuts and bruises.

The article describes them as "three grown men with jobs and families." This may be. But when they got into that canoe—and I mean this as the highest compliment—they were *guys.*

# 2

# The Biological Nature of Guys

## Important Scientific Reasons Why They Act Like Jerks

TO UNDERSTAND GUYS, it is essential to remember that, deep down inside, they are biological creatures, like jellyfish or trees, only less likely to clean the bathroom. When you see a guy in the modern urban environment, sitting at the wheel of his automobile, waiting for the traffic light to change, what you see on the *surface* is an intelligent, rational, technologically advanced being picking his nose. But if you were to probe beneath that sophisticated veneer, you would find all kinds of powerful instincts and glands and hormones and semidigested Chinese food, all of which combine to exert tremendous influence over the guy's behavior. Nowhere is this clearer than in the area of:

# ☞ *Sex.*

Although humans tend to view sex as mainly a fun recreational activity sometimes resulting in death, in nature it is a far more serious matter. Because sex is vital to the continuation of life. Granted, there are some species that have developed ways of surviving without having sex. The West Asian Wincing Lizard, for example, propagates itself entirely by adoption.

But most species must have sex to survive. And that is why, in most of nature, sex is a very grim business indeed. Take dragonflies. Next time you see two dragonflies having sex in midair, take a good look at their faces. Do they appear to be enjoying themselves? Are they smiling? Of course not. To the best of our knowledge, dragonflies don't even have *mouths.* No, they are deadly serious, because they know that if they fail to perform the sex act correctly, all the other insects will laugh at them. That's the disadvantage of doing it right out in midair.

"Dammit, Arthur," the female would say, if she had a mouth. "Why can't we just go to a motel?"

Another reason why the dragonflies are so serious about the sex act is that if they don't do it right, the female won't be able to produce any eggs, and come springtime there won't be any baby dragonflies emerging from the cocoon[1] and standing up on their cute little wobbly legs and sleepily blinking their 4,968,938,109,944 eyes and stretching their gossamer wings and edging tentatively to the edge of the tree branch and stepping off into space and SNORK getting swallowed by Mr. Wren, who has been waiting for this moment all winter.

Thus we see how important it is for dragonflies to produce a very large number of offspring, which means they have to have a *lot* of sex. This is true of most species, and usually it is up to the male to initiate the sex act.[2]

Males take this responsibility seriously. In many species, the males develop bright coloration and attend special schools where they learn complex mating rituals designed to attract females. Consider the behavior of the rare Brown-Spotted Contractor Ferret. When the male of this species spots a female, he will race around, making a noise that sounds like *"Wheep! Wheep!"* and gathering up small sticks, which he will painstakingly assemble, using dirt mixed with saliva as a sort of mortar, into a small structure shaped not unlike a Barca-Lounger. This task often takes him as long as four

---

[1] Assuming dragonflies have cocoons.
[2] Nature doesn't dare leave this up to the female, because a lot of the time she has a headache.

hours, after which the female will approach, make a noise that sounds like *"Pfah,"* then scamper off into the forest, because the last thing she needs is ugly furniture made with spit. That is why this particular ferret is so rare.

But the point is that the male is *trying.* He believes that having sex is the central biological reason for his existence. All guys do. We guys get accused of just wanting to get laid a lot, but the truth is that we have been entrusted with an extremely important responsibility—the very survival of the species—and by gosh we're going to try to carry out this responsibility, even if it means we have to try to have a lot of sex.

Don't thank us; we're just doing our job.

Guys in some species take this responsibility so seriously that they'll try to have sex with *anything.* I am looking at a page in a biology textbook with a photo caption that states: "Indiscriminate sexual behavior is common among males." Above this caption are two photographs. The first shows a guy toad trying to have sex with a *human finger.* I am not making this up. The caption states: "A male toad (*left*) clasps a finger as if it were a female of his species." And sure enough, the toad is really *wrapped* around the finger, looking very passionate, for a toad. He is so determined to have sex that he has not even noticed that his partner (a) is not, technically, a toad, and (b) is attached to an organism roughly two thousand times his size. He doesn't care! *He's getting laid!*

And he is probably already thinking about making a pass at the thumb.

But if you think *that* is an atypical example of indiscriminate sexual behavior, consider the other photograph in this biology textbook. The caption states: "An Australian buprestid beetle (*right*) attempts to copulate with a beer bottle."

Sure enough, there's the guy beetle, humping away on the side of a beer bottle that does not even *remotely* resemble a female beetle. It clearly resembles a beer bottle; in fact, it resembles an *ugly* beer bottle. But this guy beetle appears to be bonking it with great enthusiasm, and what is more, he will probably *brag* about this to the other guy beetles.

"So," is the message he will communicate, by waving his antennae in a certain boastful pattern, "guess who scored today?" And then he will nod his head[3] in a significant manner toward the beer bottle.

"Damn!" the guy beetles will indicate, waving their antennae in an envious manner. "I've been trying to get her for *months!*"

There are plenty of examples of the lengths that guys in other species will go to to have sex. I once read about

---

[3] Assuming beetles can nod.

a species of fish wherein the male is much smaller than the female, and when he mates with her, he becomes permanently stuck to her, and then she sort of absorbs him until he is actually *part of her body*, just an appendage of the female, kind of like whoever is currently married to Elizabeth Taylor. You talk about a guy giving up a *lot* for sex. The guy fish's days of hanging out with the other guys on the reef are *over*.

And let's not forget banana slugs. Actually, you're going to *want* to forget banana slugs, once you find out what they sometimes do to separate from each other after having sex, according to a fascinating book called *The Banana Slug*, which was written by Alice Bryant Harper and sent to me by alert reader John W. Glendening. This book states that banana slugs have very large sexual organs (for slugs, I mean), and sometimes, after the sex act, they remain stuck together, and in order to get themselves apart, they

> ## WARNING WARNING WARNING
>
> The U.S. Surgeon General has determined that the remainder of this sentence should not be read by guys of the male gender.

*take turns gnawing off the penis.*

So the conclusions that we can draw from this detailed survey of the wildlife kingdom is that guys in the wild, because of this great and sacred responsibility they feel to keep the species going, will:

1. Have sex with just about anything.
2. Do just about anything to have sex.

Of course human beings, as a species, are no longer subject to the kinds of threats that face animals in the wild. Thanks to modern medical advances such as anesthesia, antibiotics, and organ transplants, few human beings born in the latter half of the twentieth century have been eaten by wrens. But the basic underlying guy reproductive instincts are still there, as powerful as ever.

I am not saying here that human guys are as sexually indiscriminate as toads and beetles. I'm saying human guys are capable of being much *more* indiscriminate. Anybody who doesn't believe this should spend some time observing guys in bars. At first they will be somewhat restrained, but after a few drinks they are capable of making passes at women whom they really don't find attractive at all, or other guy's wives, or nuns, or reasonably well-groomed livestock. ("Bartender! Give this little lady here some hay!")

I'm not saying that women don't think about sex also. I'm saying that women are capable, for at least brief periods of time, of *not* thinking about sex, and that most guys are not. This is why, when an attractive woman walks past a group of guys, no matter what activity they are engaged in, they will suffer an attack of Lust-Induced Brain Freeze (LIBF):

BOMB-DISPOSAL EXPERT *(calmly but urgently):* Okay, we have fifteen seconds to bypass the timer circuit. On the count of three, I'm going to switch to auxiliary power, and I want you to short out these contacts, got it?

SECOND EXPERT: Got it.

FIRST EXPERT: Okay, one, two . . . *(An attractive woman walks by.)*

FIRST EXPERT: Whoa.

SECOND EXPERT: Yes.

FIRST EXPERT: Mmm-*MMM.*

SECOND EXPERT: YES.

FIRST EXPERT: Whoa *momma.*

SECOND EXPERT: *YESSSS.*

BOMB: Boom.

Perhaps you think I am exaggerating. Perhaps you think that intelligent guys cannot be reduced to this level of drooling idiocy by indiscriminate lust. Well, perhaps you can recall the 1988 Democratic presidential primary campaign, starring Gary Hart, who everybody agreed had a Brilliant Political Mind, which at some point must have gone through the following analytical process:

- *On the one hand, I have a very good opportunity here to become the Democratic nominee for president, and a rea-*

*sonable chance to become president of the United States, the most powerful person on Earth, capable of influencing the lives of literally billions of people and changing the course of history.*

- *On the other hand, I can have a HOT BABE sit in my lap.*

No contest! Lust-Induced Brain Freeze triumphs again!

I want to stress here that I am *not* saying that guys are stupid. I am saying that, because of subtle and extremely complex biochemical reactions taking place in their bodies, guys *act* stupid.

The main ingredient in these reactions, as you are no doubt aware, is a substance that guys contain called testosterone.[4] But what you may *not* be aware of is that testosterone is actually illegal. I found this out when I got a letter from a reader named Richard Watkins, who is a physician and who sent me a shocking medical document concerning the federal Anabolic Steroids Control Act.

Steroids are substances that some guys put in their bodies in an effort to develop bulging, rippling, sharply defined muscles like the ones Michael Keaton wore when he was Batman. This is foolish, because women are not attracted to rippling, sharply defined muscles. Women prefer a type of male physique that is known,

---

[4]From the Greek words *testo*, meaning "stuff," and *sterone*, meaning "that guys contain."

in body-building circles, as "the humor writer." This is a softer, more-rounded, aerodynamic shape, similar to the one used in the popular Ford Taurus station wagon. This physique has inspired a whole line of mature-guy casual pants, which go by the name "Dockers" because it was not considered a shrewd marketing move to come right out and call them "Pants for the Bigger-Butted Man."

But back to steroids. They have bad side effects, although it took medical researchers many years to discover this. They'd get a bunch of steroid users together and say, "Okay, anybody having bad side effects, raise your hand!" The steroid users would strain and grunt like water buffaloes in labor, but due to their extreme muscularity they couldn't raise their hands above their waists. Many of them must press elevator buttons with their foreheads.

The result was that medical researchers had no idea what kinds of problems steroids were causing until one day when they happened to ask for oral responses. Then they discovered the awful truth: steroids can cause men to develop thick Austrian accents. This is what happened to Arnold Schwarzenegger, who was actually born and raised in Topeka, Kansas, and spoke like a regular American until he used steroids to build his body up to the point where he was legally classified by the U.S. Census Bureau as "construction equipment."

So anyway, the government is cracking down on steroids. I thought this was a fine idea until I got Dr. Watkins's letter, which was written on a hospital physical-examination form, in the section headed "Chief Complaint and Present Illness."

"Here I am," Dr. Watkins wrote, "sitting around in my doctor suit waiting for an emergency to happen, and suddenly I get a memo: ON FEB. 27, 1991, TESTOSTERONE WAS DECLARED A CONTROLLED SUBSTANCE, LIKE HEROIN."

My immediate reaction was to think that Dr. Watkins had been wearing his stethoscope way too tight. But it turns out he's telling the absolute truth. With his letter, he enclosed a document from the Group Health Cooperative of Puget Sound, listing various types of anabolic steroids now controlled by the federal government, and testosterone is on the list.

This presents a serious legal problem, because *many* guys, including several known Supreme Court members, are walking around with testosterone in their possession. They can't help it. As Dr. Watkins put it, in medical terminology, testosterone is "a substance exuded by your you-know organs, hereinafter your Ralphs."

So as I interpret this document—and bear in mind that I applied to law school *twice*—it is basically against the law to be a guy. This makes sense to me. Testosterone is a dangerous thing. Aside from causing indiscriminate sexual behavior, it can result in:

## Guys Acting Macho

Guys start acting macho at an early age. Any parent will tell you that girl babies will generally display a wide-eyed curiosity about the world, whereas boy babies will generally try to destroy it. Girl toddlers will work hard to communicate with and imitate the behavior of other family members; boy toddlers will imagine that they are large meat-eating dinosaurs and stomp around the house in their disposable diapers, trying to bite the dog.

Of course I am talking about very young guys here. As guys grow older, and produce more testosterone, they become less mature. This is especially true when they're in control of automobiles. One morning I was driving in Miami on Interstate 95, which should have a sign that says:

---

WARNING
EXTREMELY HIGH TESTOSTERONE LEVELS
NEXT 15 MILES

---

In the left lane, one behind the other, were two well-dressed middle-aged men, both driving luxury telephone-equipped automobiles. They looked like responsible business executives, probably named Roger, with good jobs and nice families and male pattern baldness, the kind of guys whose most violent physical activity, on an average day, is stapling.

They were driving normally, except that the guy in front, Roger One, was thoughtlessly going only about sixty-five miles an hour, which in Miami is the speed limit normally observed inside car washes. So Roger Two pulled up behind until the two cars were approximately one electron apart, and honked his horn.

Of course Roger One was not about to stand for *that.* You let a guy honk at you, and you are basically admitting that he has a bigger stapler. So Roger One stomped on his brakes, forcing Roger Two to swerve onto the shoulder, where, showing amazing presence of mind in an emergency, he was able to make obscene gestures *with both hands.*

At this point both Rogers accelerated to approximately 147 miles per hour and began weaving violently from lane to lane through dense rush-hour traffic, each risking numerous lives in an effort to get in front of the other, screaming and getting spit all over their walnut dashboards. I quickly lost sight of them, but I bet neither one backed down. Their coworkers probably wondered what happened to them. "Where the heck is Roger?" they probably said later that morning, unaware that, even as they spoke, the dueling Rogers, still only inches apart, were approaching the Canadian border.

This is not unusual guy behavior. One time in a

Washington, D.C., traffic jam I saw two guys, also driving nice cars, reach a point where their lanes were supposed to merge. But neither one would yield, so they very slowly—we are talking maybe one mile per hour—*drove into each other*. It was the world's most avoidable accident, but these guys had no choice. Testosterone made them crash into each other, just as, in the animal kingdom, testosterone controls the behavior of male elks, who, instead of simply flipping a coin, will bang their heads against each other for hours to see who gets to mate with the female elk, who is on the sidelines, filing her nails and wondering how she ever got hooked up with such a moron species, until eventually she gets bored and wanders off to bed. Meanwhile the guy elks keep banging into each other until one of them finally "wins," although at this point his brain, which was not exactly a steel trap to begin with, is so badly damaged that, in his confusion, he will mate with the first object he encounters, including shrubbery.

This is of course the great irony of macho behavior: Women never seemed to be impressed by it. You rarely hear women say things like, "Norm, when that vending machine failed to give you a Three Musketeers bar and you punched it so hard that you broke your hand and we had to go to the hospital instead of to my best friend's daughter's wedding, I became so filled with lust for you that I nearly tore off all my clothes right there in the emergency room." No, women are far more likely to say: "Norm, you have the brains of an Odor Eater."

No guy is immune to testosterone pressure. Once in New York City I was in a car driven by Calvin "Bud" Trillin, a great guy, a great writer, and one of the most civilized, courteous, and urbane people I know. He was waiting for another driver to pull out of a parking space, when a third driver started to pull past us. I thought this driver was just trying to pass, and so did Bud's wife, Alice, but Bud was certain the driver was trying to get his parking space, so he honked his horn and gestured angrily. This led to the following exchange between Alice and Bud:

ALICE: Bud, he just wants to get past.

BUD *(raising his voice):* He's a SHIT POT, Alice, and he WANTS MY SPACE.

Fortunately the other driver kept going, which meant that Bud did not have to run him down. Bud was displaying the territorial urge, there. This also dates back to primitive times, when guys would need a certain amount of land so they could have somewhere to hunt, fish, spit, etc. Of course this was the Upper East Side of Manhattan, and the parking spot was not exactly teeming with game. It was more teeming with Marlboro butts. But territory is territory, for guys. Bud was driven by the same powerful instinct that causes guy dogs to mark off their territory by peeing on it.

Show a guy dog anything—Mount McKinley, the Gobi Desert, the Parthenon—and his immediate reaction will be: "Hey! I better pee on this!" Your basic guy dog firmly believes that if he pees on enough territory, he will be declared Dominant Male Dog of the Entire Earth and receive a plaque plus valuable dog prizes, such as a bag of dead squirrels.

This is basically the same instinct that determines U.S. foreign policy, except that instead of peeing on foreign countries, we give them money or drop bombs on them, sometimes simultaneously. Thus we see that testosterone can lead to some very destructive forms of male behavior, the two worst being:

1. War
2. Do-it-yourself projects

It's a well-known fact that a male with even a moderate testosterone level would rather drill a hole in his hand (which he probably will) than admit, especially to his spouse, that he cannot do something himself. Put an ordinary husband on the Space Shuttle, and within minutes he'll be telling his spouse that by God he'll repair the retro thruster modules, because if you call in NASA they'll just charge you an arm and a leg. I personally have destroyed numerous perfectly good rooms by undertaking frenzied testosterone-induced efforts to fix them up despite the fact that I have the manual dexterity of an oyster. Hundreds of years from now, archaeologists will look at my home-improvement projects and say: "This civilization was apparently wiped out by a terrible natural disaster involving spackle."

We will explore some of these issues in more detail later in this book, but the point I am trying to make here is that when we see guys acting in certain guy ways, we must not judge them too harshly. We must view them the same way we view any other creatures of nature, such as snakes. They do things that seem inappropriate in a civilized world, but they are only following behavioral patterns that were embedded in them eons ago. If we are patient and understanding with them, if we seek to understand what "makes them tick," we can succeed in modifying their behavior and bringing them more "in tune" with modern society.

I'm talking about snakes here. Guys are hopeless.

# 3

# The Social Development of Guys

## Nature Alone Should Not Take the Rap

SO FAR in this book I have shown, using extensive scientific documentation,[1] that there are powerful underlying biological reasons why guys act the way they do, as opposed to acting like human beings.

But society also plays a role in determining guy behavior. This process begins right at birth, when the tiny guy baby is still emerging from the mother, and the doctor tells her that it's a boy, and she, in a

[1] Available on request.

classic expression of maternal joy, responds, "ARGGHHHHHHHH." She is not feeling so great, because the baby is not *that* tiny, compared with the orifice that it is emerging from. Childbirth, as a strictly physical phenomenon, is comparable to driving a United Parcel truck through an inner tube.

But my point is that even then, as the male baby is barely entering the outside world, he starts to become indoctrinated into the ways of guyness, because of the way he will be treated by his parents, particularly his father. Some fathers will attempt to teach their sons to play catch right there in the delivery room. ("No, son! Always catch the ball *away* from your umbilical cord!") This process continues when the baby guy gets home, and his parents give him a bunch of stereotypically male toys to play with. It is sad but true that even today, boy babies are generally given toys that stress power and dominance, such as trucks and planes and trains; whereas girl babies generally get toys that stress nurturing and sacrifice, such as dolls with names like Baby Puke-On-U.

It's hard to avoid falling into the stereotype-toy trap. When my son, Rob, was born, my philosophy was that he should have only politically correct, environmentally sound, gender-neutral toys, such as a spinning top carved out of nonendangered wood or recycled tofu. Sincerely determined to purchase something along these lines when I went to the Toys "Я" "A" Big

Industry store, I am sincerely embarrassed to report that what I actually purchased was a radio-controlled tank. I couldn't help myself. This was a really *neat* tank. It had a working turret and real treads, so it could turn on a dime and climb right over various obstacles, such as books or pillows or my son, Rob, who, being a small infant with basically the same motor skills as a watermelon, was unable to operate this tank personally. So I had to operate it for him, which I did at every opportunity, because he seemed to enjoy it, as was indicated by the increase in his drool output.

This is also how I could tell that he liked the electric train.

Thus we see that even sensitive and concerned parents such as myself can contribute to the guy-ization of a male infant. But I think it would happen anyway, because little boys just naturally seem to be crazy for power. For example, from early on, Rob loved big trucks. He loved them even before he could pronounce either "big" or "truck." When he saw a big truck, he'd say something that sounded like "bee fut." He said it a lot, because he was *obsessed.* He only had eyes for trucks. We'd be in midtown Manhattan shortly before Christmas, walking beneath spectacular skyscrapers, past delightful animated store-window displays, with music playing everywhere and Santa Claus clanging his bell on every corner, and Rob's attention would be totally focused on: a garbage truck.

"Bee fut!" he'd tell me, pointing at it.

"Bee fut!" he'd inform random pedestrians.

"Bee fut!" he'd state to the world in general, repeating it 1,753 times, in case any unfortunate person might be unaware of this amazing development. And I'd have to stand there in the cold for fifteen minutes, admiring this stinking, crud-encrusted hulk and agreeing over and over that, fut-wise, it was extremely bee.

Then came the dinosaur phase. Rob loved dinosaurs even more than he loved trucks, and I don't think this was because dinosaurs were fascinating and diverse creatures whose fossilized remains can teach us much about the rich biological history of our still-mysterious planet. I think he loved them because they could stomp an enemy flatter than a cheap pizza. Power, that's what dinosaurs symbolized: We're talking about massive, forty-foot-high creatures with fearsome claws and massive jaws; creatures that enjoyed total physical domination over every other life-form; creatures that *did not have to go to bed unless they felt like it.* Many a weekday night I would be exhausted, desperate to fall asleep, but unable to do so because a short but fierce *Tyrannosaurus rex* was raging through the house, waving its pacifier around angrily, declaring that it was not at *all* tired.

So I suppose it was inevitable that Rob would be interested in power-and-dominance toys. But I want to stress, as a fundamentally nonviolent person who has never owned any form of weapon, that I did *not* buy him toy guns. I'm not saying he didn't *have* any toy guns; in fact, by the time he was four, he had enough toy guns to conquer a toy nation the size of France.[2] I don't know where they came from. They just appeared in my house, and in the houses of all my nonviolent, son-having friends. I think maybe the Gun Fairy finds out where little boys live and comes around at night, dressed in camouflage, scattering battery-operated Nuclear Death Rayguns everywhere.[3]

The TV cartoon shows aimed at little boys don't help, either. They're infested with characters who have biceps the size of prize-winning hogs and names like Commander Brock Gonad and His Hard Punchers of Justice. In an effort to please government regulatory agencies and child-psychology experts, these shows *pretend* to involve uplifting themes such as racial tolerance, ecological awareness, and nonviolence, but in fact they almost always involve macho behavior:

COMMANDER GONAD: Uh-oh, Sarge, looks like we have company!

SERGEANT STEROID: It's Anthrax, the evil villain from the planet Polluto! With no concern whatsoever for the environment! And it looks like he has . . .

ANTHRAX *(in evil voice):* That's right, you fools! I have

[2]Come to think of it, he probably could have conquered the *real* France.
[3]Needless to say, the Gun Fairy *never* leaves batteries.

the Giant Atomic Fluorocarbon-Emitting Hairspray Container of Doom, and I am going to spritz the *entire Earth* and destroy every living thing on it!

SERGEANT STEROID: *Uh*-oh! That would mean . . .

ANTHRAX: Yes! That would mean *the extinction of the Spotted Owl HAHAHAHA!*

COMMANDER GONAD: We've got to stop him! By nonviolent means if at all possible! Listen, Anthrax! Be reasonable!

ANTHRAX: No!

COMMANDER GONAD: Okay, then! *(He beats the shit out of Anthrax.)*

SERGEANT STEROID: Whew! That was a close one!

COMMANDER GONAD: Yes! Every species is important, which is why we need to protect our planet and recycle whenever possible and eat hearty nutritious meals including the breakfast cereals advertised relentlessly on this program!

SERGEANT STEROID: Part of this complete breakfast! By the way, action figures based on our characters are available in toy stores everywhere! Sold separately!

COMMANDER GONAD: Collect them all! Speaking of licensed characters, look who's here! It's Corporal Token!

CORPORAL TOKEN: That's right! Please note that I am an African American!

COMMANDER GONAD: Right on, "homes!" "What it is!" And here's Lieutenant Woman!

LIEUTENANT WOMAN: Speaking of owls, please note that I have an anatomically impossible set of hooters! *(General Laughter)*

This is the kind of show my son watched. And don't tell me that it could have been prevented by not allowing him to watch television. Modern children don't need the medium of a TV set. The human race has evolved to the point where children can receive broadcast waves directly from the atmosphere, just as they can program VCRs and set digital watches without reading the instructions.

For a couple of years my son was *deeply* into a TV-show hero and licensed character named "He-Man." Rob had He-Man sheets on his bed and wore He-Man underwear.[4] Of course he also had a vast collection of He-Man action figures, which were ludicrously muscular and disfigured in various ways to reflect their special individual powers, reflected by their names. One of them had insectlike wings that enabled him to fly; this was "Buzz-Off." Another one had a skunklike stripe down his back and gave off an unpleasant aroma; his name was "Stinkor" (I am not making up these action figures).

At one point I believe I had more money invested in He-Man action figures than in my Individual Retirement Account. Rob was determined to collect all of the

---

[4]So does Sylvester Stallone.

figures, which was of course impossible, because no matter how many I bought, the people who created these things—I imagined them as being a bunch of pudgy balding guys whose idea of a tough physical challenge would be placing a conference call—kept making more. It became difficult for me to keep track of which ones Rob already had and which new ones he wanted the most. Around Christmas and birthday time I spent long periods in the He-Man aisle of Toys "Я" Us, scratching my head at the vast array of figures, sometimes consulting with other parents:

ME: Excuse me, but is Man-at-Arms the one that can shoot out a hook with a rope attached to it and hook onto things?

SECOND PARENT: No, I think Man-at-Arms is the sidekick for Skeletor.

THIRD PARENT: No, Man-at-Arms can't be Skeletor's sidekick. Man-at-Arms is a *good* guy. He's *He-Man's* sidekick.

SECOND PARENT: Then which one is Skeletor's sidekick?

THIRD PARENT: I think his name is something like DungHeap.

ME: Is he the one who squirts brown glop from either end?

SECOND PARENT: No, I think that's WormLord.

THIRD PARENT: Is he good?

FOURTH PARENT: I don't think so, because he's friends

with what's-his-name, the one who has a scary face and giant powerful claw arms, yet fears melted butter.

FIFTH PARENT: Lob-Stor.

SECOND PARENT: Let's all go to a bar.

That's what we should have done, anyway. But instead we brought more He-Man action figures home. The house was infested with them. Wherever you turned, you'd find them—on the floor, on the furniture, clinging to curtains, standing defiantly on top of the toilet seat, etc. It was forbidden to move any of them, because Rob had carefully positioned each one to play a role in a gigantic action-figure battle that lasted, to the best of my recollection, three years.

The battle consisted mainly of arch-enemies He-Man and Skeletor making dramatic statements to each other in Rob's deepest four-year-old voice, using the stilted language popular with hack cartoon-dialogue writers:

SKELETOR: He-Man, you shall die, and Castle Greyskull shall be *all mine!*

HE-MAN: I think not! *(He hits Skeletor, knocking him ten feet, which is the equivalent of about 250 action-figure feet.)*

SKELETOR: You shall pay for that, He-Man!

HE-MAN: I think not! *(He knocks Skeletor another 250 feet.)*

Even though Skeletor was the most evil being in the universe, I felt kind of sorry for him. He took a tremendous amount of physical punishment. He got thrown out of windows. He got slammed in doors. He got run over by a tricycle. He got frozen solid in the freezer. He got dunked in Rob's beets. But he kept coming back for more.[5]

My point here is that the toys marketed for boys, like the TV shows, tend to encourage the boys' already aggressive nature, which could be why boys spend so much time acting like what trained professional psychologists call "jerks." Or it could be that boys are born with some kind of jerk gene, and the toy and TV people are merely cashing in on this. Whatever the cause, I know I spent a lot of time envying parents of girls. I'd take my son and his friends to a Burger King, and I'd see a table of little girls, and they'd be eating and talking, just like miniature humans. Whereas my son and his friends seemed to have some kind of nervous-system linkage between their mouths and their hands, so that they could not chew without punching. Eating with them was as relaxing as amateur eyeball surgery.

"Stop punching," I'd say.

They'd try to stop, sometimes succeeding for as long as .00014 seconds. Then the Punch Reflex would overwhelm their tiny mental circuits.

"Stop punching!" I'd repeat.

---

[5]I mean more punishment. Not more beets.

"We're not punching!" they'd say, punching.

"YOU ARE TOO PUNCHING!!" I'd shout, spewing out pieces of semichewed hamburger. "I CAN *SEE* YOU PUNCHING!! NOW STOP PUNCHING!! AND STOP BLOWING BUBBLES IN YOUR MILKSHAKES!! AND STOP SQUIRTING THE KETCHUP PACKETS AT EACH OTHER!! JUST EAT!!"

They'd look at me as though I were insane. Their feeling was, if you were only going to *eat*, what was the point of going to a restaurant?

Then I'd look over at the table of little girls, who'd be chatting and thoughtfully passing each other the napkins, and I would wonder how we ever permitted *my* gender to get control of, for example, the government.

At this point you are saying, "Dave, in all fairness, there is more to boys than just punching. As they enter preadolescence and prepare to accept their roles as productive and independent members of society, they begin to display many other facets to their personalities, such as the burping facet and the farting facet."

True. Looking back on my own childhood, I would estimate that my friends and I spent about 75 percent of our waking hours from fifth through eighth grades burping, farting, or laughing hysterically when somebody else burped or farted. We never grew tired of these activities; they invariably struck us as life-threateningly funny. One of my friends, Harry Tompkins,[6] had developed the ability to burp *and* fart on command,[7] and we considered this to be a far greater achievement than the polio vaccine.

Virtually all of my memories of Boy Scouts involve farting. I spent several years in the Boy Scouts, ultimately attaining the rank of Second Class, but I can't remember the Morse Code, or how to hang your backpack from a rope so the raccoons can't get your food, or how to start a fire by rubbing pine cones together, or how to tie important tactical knots with names like the "sheepskank." What I can remember is being out in the woods on scout-troop camping trips, at 1:30 A.M., lying in a sleeping bag in a tent with three other guys, none of us even *close* to falling asleep due to the fact that we were entertaining ourselves by ritualistically telling jokes that we had all heard upwards of four hundred times, such as:

"What'd you have for breakfast?"
"Pea soup."
"What'd you have for lunch?"
"Pea soup."
"What'd you have for supper?"
"Pea soup."
"What'd you do all night?"

[6]Harry, if you're out there: Hi, and I hope you haven't become a federal judge or anything.
[7]The command was: "Harry! Burp and fart!"

"Pee soup."
(Laughter, followed by shouts of "BE QUIET!" and "GO
TO SLEEP!" from the scoutmaster's tent.)

So we'd be lying there, trying to giggle as quietly as
possible, and one of the guys—probably as a result of
eating our usual Boy-Scout-camping-trip food, which
consisted of semi-warmed baked beans mixed with
Hershey's chocolate and Tang—would have some kind
of gaseous nuclear chain reaction in his bowels, and
there would be a sound like

# BWAAARRRRRPPPPPPP

and flames would come shooting out of the victim's
sleeping bag and the tent walls would bulge violently
outward, and the other three of us guys, in a desperate
effort to escape before the tent was filled with the
Deadly Blue Cloud, would lunge for the tent flap, still
inside our sleeping bags, all trying to get out simultaneously, so that, from the outside, the tent looked like
some bizarre alien space pod giving birth to giant
crazed green worms.

"GAS ATTACK!" we'd shout, causing the startled
raccoons to drop our Hershey bars.

"BE QUIET!" the scoutmaster's tent would shout,
but by now we were totally out of control, rolling
around on the ground, howling, setting off chain reactions of laughter and fart noises in the other tents.

Boy Scouts: It made me the leader I am today.

Of course what I'm describing here is the humor of preadolescent guys. As guys grow older and become more mature, their humor begins to reflect and ultimately revolve around a fundamental and universal human theme that will remain the focal point of the guys' existence for the remainder of their lives, namely, their private organs. Guys are absolutely fascinated with their privates. There is no explaining this. I mean, women also happen to have sexual organs; in fact they have dozens of them, highly complex biological units that, if unrolled, would extend for miles, and that are capable of performing astounding feats of reproduction. Yet you never hear women giving their organs pet names, or viewing them as a major source of humor. But put two guys together, and before long they'll be exchanging private-parts jokes, even if they are highly sophisticated guys such as John Updike or myself.

Women generally do not see the hilarity in this type of joke. I attribute this to a lack of humor sophistication on their part, caused by the fact that, for some reason, women do not dedicate large sectors of their brains exclusively to the appreciation and storage of jokes. Most guys *have* done this with their brains, which is why they can remember jokes they learned in the third grade, whereas they can't always remember exactly, down to the last digit, how many of their parents are still living.

Guys are deeply interested in jokes, as you know if

you have ever been in contact with the vast, high-speed Global Guy Joke Network. This is a worldwide complex of millions of dedicated guys who, the instant they hear a new joke, are willing to drop whatever they're doing, especially if it's work, and immediately pass the joke along to other guys all over the world at company expense. Guys take the responsibility for joke-propagation very seriously, and they pride themselves on their ability to develop and transmit jokes in response to major tragedies such as the Space Shuttle disaster or the Branch Davidian cult compound fire. When events such as these occur, the U.S. economy is virtually shut down by concerned guys using every available phone, fax, modem, satellite, etc., to transmit urgent new tragedy-related jokes, such as how you pick up women in Waco, Texas.[8] In July of 1991, within minutes after Milwaukee police revealed that Jeffrey Dahmer had been keeping enough body parts in his apartment to form a complete football team including field-goal unit, there were Dahmer jokes flying all over the world. You could have gone to a remote area of the Amazon River basin, where there is no electricity or phone service and all long-distance communication is accomplished via drums, and you would have heard the following exchange reverberating through the rain forest:

[8]With a Dustbuster.

FIRST DRUM: BEAT BEAT BEAT BEAT. *(Say, did you hear what they found in Jeffrey Dahmer's freezer?)*

SECOND DRUM: BEAT BEAT BEAT. *(No, what did they find?)*

FIRST DRUM: BEAT BEAT BEAT BEAT BEAT. *(Ben and Jerry.)*

SECOND DRUM: BEAT! *(Har!)*

THIRD DRUM: BEAT BEAT BEAT! BEAT BEAT BEAT BEAT BEAT! *(Hey you guys! Stop telling jokes on company drums!)*

Why do guys do this? Why do they make fun of horrible tragedies? Could it be that they are trying to deny the anguish and fear they feel when these tragedies force them to confront the terrifying fragility of human existence? Don't make me laugh. Guys do this because they're *sick.* This is also why they think it's funny to hurl moons at nuns or tip cows over or stay up all night on the eve of a wedding, taking the groom's car completely apart and reassembling it inside the happy couple's new fourteenth-floor apartment. I am not apologizing for this kind of behavior, mind you; I happen to find it childish and unappealing, and I wish that guys would just for God's sake *grow up.* I am certain that you feel the same way, so I will not burden you with the stupid and tasteless joke about the guy who catches the fish with the seventeen-inch penis.[9]

---

[9]There is no such joke. Made you look.

# 4

## Tips for Women

### How to Have a Relationship with a Guy

CONTRARY TO  what many women believe, it's fairly easy to develop a long-term, stable, intimate, and mutually fulfilling relationship with a guy. Of course this guy has to be a Labrador retriever. With human guys, it's extremely difficult. This is because guys don't really grasp what women mean by the term *relationship*.

Let's say a guy named Roger is attracted to a woman named Elaine. He asks her out to a movie; she accepts; they have a pretty good time. A few nights later he asks her out to dinner, and again they enjoy themselves.

They continue to see each other regularly, and after a while neither one of them is seeing anybody else.

And then, one evening when they're driving home, a thought occurs to Elaine, and, without really thinking, she says it aloud: "Do you realize that, as of tonight, we've been seeing each other for exactly six months?"

And then there is silence in the car. To Elaine, it seems like a very loud silence. She thinks to herself: Geez, I wonder if it bothers him that I said that. Maybe he's been feeling confined by our relationship; maybe he thinks I'm trying to push him into some kind of obligation that he doesn't want, or isn't sure of.

And Roger is thinking: Gosh. *Six months.*

And Elaine is thinking: But, hey, *I'm* not so sure I want this kind of relationship, either. Sometimes I wish *I* had a little more space, so I'd have time to think about whether I really want us to keep going the way we are, moving steadily toward . . . I mean, where *are* we going? Are we just going to keep seeing each other at this level of intimacy? Are we heading toward *marriage?* Toward *children?* Toward a *lifetime* together? Am I ready for that level of commitment? Do I really even *know* this person?

And Roger is thinking: . . . so that means it was . . . let's see . . . *February* when we started going out, which was right after I had the car at the dealer's, which means . . . lemme check the odometer . . . *Whoa!* I am *way* overdue for an oil change here.

And Elaine is thinking: He's upset. I can see it on his face. Maybe I'm reading this completely wrong. Maybe he wants *more* from our relationship, *more* intimacy, *more* commitment; maybe he has sensed—even before *I* sensed it—that I was feeling some reservations. Yes, I bet that's it. That's why he's so reluctant to say anything about his own feelings: He's afraid of being rejected.

And Roger is thinking: And I'm gonna have them look at the transmission again. I don't care *what* those morons say, it's still not shifting right. And they better not try to blame it on the cold weather this time. *What cold weather?* It's eighty-seven degrees out, and this thing is shifting like a goddamn *garbage truck,* and I paid those incompetent thieving cretin bastards *six hundred dollars.*

And Elaine is thinking: He's angry. And I don't blame him. I'd be angry, too. God, I feel so *guilty,* putting him through this, but I can't help the way I feel. I'm just not *sure.*

And Roger is thinking: They'll probably say it's only a ninety-day warranty. That's exactly what they're gonna say, the scumballs.

And Elaine is thinking: Maybe I'm just too idealistic, waiting for a knight to come riding up on his white horse, when I'm sitting right next to a perfectly good person, a person I enjoy being with, a person I truly do care about, a person who seems to truly care about me. A person who is in pain because of my self-centered, schoolgirl romantic fantasy.

And Roger is thinking: Warranty? They want a warranty? *I'll* give them a goddamn warranty. I'll take their warranty and stick it right up their . . .

"Roger," Elaine says aloud.

"What?" says Roger, startled.

"Please don't torture yourself like this," she says, her eyes beginning to brim with tears. "Maybe I should never have . . . Oh *God*, I feel so . . ." *(She breaks down, sobbing.)*

"What?" says Roger.

"I'm such a fool," Elaine sobs. "I mean, I know there's no knight. I really know that. It's silly. There's no knight, and there's no horse."

"There's no horse?" says Roger.

"You think I'm a fool, don't you," Elaine says.

"No!" says Roger, glad to finally know the correct answer.

"It's just that . . . It's that I . . . I need some time," Elaine says.

*(There is a fifteen-second pause while Roger, thinking as fast as he can, tries to come up with a safe response. Finally he comes up with one that he thinks might work.)*

"Yes," he says.

*(Elaine, deeply moved, touches his hand.)*

"Oh, Roger, do you really feel that way?" she says.

"What way?" says Roger.

"That way about time," says Elaine.

"Oh," says Roger. "Yes."

*(Elaine turns to face him and gazes deeply into his eyes, causing him to become very nervous about what she might say next, especially if it involves a horse. At last she speaks.)*

"Thank you, Roger," she says.

"Thank *you*," says Roger.

Then he takes her home, and she lies on her bed, a conflicted, tortured soul, and weeps until dawn, whereas when Roger gets back to his place, he opens a bag of Doritos, turns on the TV, and immediately becomes deeply involved in a rerun of a tennis match between two Czechoslovakians he has never heard of. A tiny voice in the far recesses of his mind tells him that something major was going on back there in the car, but he is pretty sure there is no way he would ever understand *what*, and so he figures it's better if he doesn't think about it. (This is also Roger's policy regarding world hunger.)

The next day Elaine will call her closest friend, or perhaps two of them, and they will talk about this situation for six straight hours. In painstaking detail, they will analyze everything she said and everything he said, going over it time and time again, exploring every word, expression, and gesture for nuances of meaning, considering every possible ramification. They will continue to discuss this subject, off and on, for weeks, maybe months, never reaching any definite conclusions, but never getting bored with it, either.

Meanwhile, Roger, while playing racquetball one day with a mutual friend of his and Elaine's, will pause just before serving, frown, and say: "Norm, did Elaine ever own a horse?"

We're not talking about different wavelengths here. We're talking about different *planets*, in completely different *solar systems*. Elaine cannot communicate meaningfully with Roger about their relationship any more than she can meaningfully play chess with a duck. Because the sum total of Roger's thinking on this particular topic is as follows:

*Huh?*

Women have a lot of trouble accepting this. Despite millions of years of overwhelming evidence to the contrary, women are convinced that guys must spend a certain amount of time thinking about the relationship. How could they not? How could a guy see another human being day after day, night after night, sharing countless hours with this person, becoming physically intimate—how can a guy be doing these things and *not* be thinking about their relationship? This is what women figure.

They are wrong. A guy in a relationship is like an ant standing on top of a truck tire. The ant is aware, on a very basic level, that something large is there, but he cannot even dimly comprehend what this thing is, or the nature of his involvement with it. And if the truck starts moving, and the tire starts to roll, the ant will sense that something important is happening, but right up until he rolls around to the bottom and is squashed into a small black blot, the only distinct thought that will form in his tiny brain will be, and I quote,

*Huh?*

Which is exactly what Roger will think when Elaine explodes with fury at him when he commits one of the endless series of petty offenses, such as asking her sister out, that guys are always committing in relationships because they have virtually no clue that they are in one.

"How *could* he?" Elaine will ask her best friends. "What was he thinking?"

The answer is, He *wasn't* thinking, in the sense that women mean the word. He can't: He doesn't have the appropriate type of brain. He has a guy brain, which is basically an analytical, problem-solving type of organ. It likes things to be definite and measurable and specific. It's not comfortable with nebulous and imprecise relationship-type concepts such as *love* and *need* and *trust*. If the guy brain has to form an opinion about another person, it prefers to form that opinion based on something concrete about the person, such as his or her earned-run average.

So the guy brain is not well-suited to grasping relationships. But it's good at analyzing and solving mechanical problems. For example, if a couple owns a house, and they want to repaint it so they can sell it, it will probably be the guy who will take charge of this project. He will methodically take the necessary measurements, calculate the total surface area, and determine the per-gallon coverage capacity of the paint; then, using his natural analytical and mathematical skills, he will apply himself to the problem of figuring out a good excuse not to paint the house.

"It's too humid," he'll say. Or: "I've read that prospective buyers are actually attracted more to a house with a lot of exterior dirt." Guys simply have a natural flair for this kind of problem-solving. That's why we always have guys in charge of handling the federal budget deficit.

But the point I'm trying to make is that, if you're a woman, and you want to have a successful relationship with a guy, the Number One Tip to remember is:

1. **Never assume that the guy understands that you and he have a relationship.**

The guy will not realize this on his own. You have to plant the idea in his brain by constantly making subtle references to it in your everyday conversation, such as:

- "Roger, would you mind passing me a Sweet 'n' Low, inasmuch as we have a relationship?"
- "Wake up, Roger! There's a prowler in the den and we have a relationship! You and I do, I mean."
- "Good news, Roger! The gynecologist says we're going to have our fourth child, which will serve as yet another indication that we have a relationship!"
- "Roger, inasmuch as this plane is crashing and we probably have only about a minute to live, I want you to know that we've had a wonderful fifty-three years of marriage together, which clearly constitutes a relationship."

Never let up, women. Pound away relentlessly at this concept, and eventually it will start to penetrate the guy's brain. Some day he might even start thinking about it on his own. He'll be talking with some other guys about women, and, out of the blue, he'll say, "Elaine and I, we have, ummm . . . We have, ahhh . . . We . . . We have this *thing*."

And he will sincerely mean it.

The next relationship-enhancement tip is:

**2. Do not expect the guy to make a hasty commitment.**

By "hasty," I mean, "within your lifetime." Guys are *extremely* reluctant to make commitments. This is because they never feel *ready*.

"I'm sorry," guys are always telling women, "but I'm just not ready to make a commitment." Guys are in a permanent state of nonreadiness. If guys were turkey breasts, you could put them in a 350-degree oven on July Fourth, and they *still* wouldn't be done in time for Thanksgiving.

Women have a lot of trouble understanding this. Women ask themselves: How can a guy say he's "not ready" to make a permanent commitment to a woman with whom he is obviously compatible; a woman whom he has been seeing for years; a woman who once drove *his* dog to the veterinarian in *her* new car when it (the dog) started making unusual stomach noises and then barfing prolifically after eating an entire birthday cake, including candles, that *she* made from scratch for *him* (the guy), the result being that her car will smell like a stadium rest room for the next five years, at the end of which this guy will probably still say he's "not ready"? And how come this same guy was somehow capable, at age seven, of committing himself to a lifelong, passionate, win-or-lose relationship with the Kansas City Royals, who have never so much as sent him a card?

A lot of women have concluded that the problem is that guys, as a group, have the emotional maturity of hamsters. No, this is not the case. A hamster is much more capable of making a lasting commitment to a woman, especially if she gives it those little food pellets.

Whereas a guy, in a relationship, will consume the pellets of companionship, and he will run on the exercise wheel of lust; but as soon as he senses that the door of commitment is about to close and trap him in the wire cage of true intimacy, he'll squirm out, scamper across the kitchen floor of uncertainty and hide under the refrigerator of nonreadiness.[1]

This is natural behavior. Guys are born with a fundamental, genetically transmitted mental condition known to psychologists as: The Fear That If You Get Attached to a Woman, Some Unattached Guy, Somewhere, Will Be Having More Fun Than You. This is why all married guys assume that all unmarried guys lead lives of constant excitement involving hot tubs full of naked international fashion models; whereas in fact for most unmarried guys, the climax of the typical evening is watching an infomercial for Hair-in-a-Spray-Can while eating onion dip straight from the container. (This is also true of married guys, although statistically they are far more likely to be using a spoon.)

So guys are extremely reluctant to make commitments, or even to take any steps that might *lead* to commitments. This is why, when a guy goes out on a date with a woman and finds himself really liking her, he often will demonstrate his affection by avoiding her for the rest of his life.

[1] I am a professional writer. Do not try these metaphors at home.

Women are puzzled by this. "I don't *understand*," they say. "We had such a great time! Why doesn't he *call?*"

The reason is that the guy, using the linear guy thought process, has realized that if he takes her out again, he'll probably like her even more, so he'll take her out *again*, and eventually they'll fall in love with each other, and they'll get married, and they'll have children, and then they'll have grandchildren, and eventually they'll retire and take a trip around the world, and they'll be walking hand-in-hand on some spectacular beach in the South Pacific, reminiscing about the lifetime of experiences they've shared together, and then several naked international fashion models will walk up and invite him to join them in a hot tub, and *he won't be able to do it.*

This is Basic Guy Logic. And it leads us to our final and most important tip for women who wish to have a successful relationship with a guy:

**3. Don't make the guy feel threatened.**

Guys are easily threatened by the tiniest hint that they have become somehow obligated, so you need to learn to give soothing, nonthreatening responses, especially in certain dangerous situations, as shown in the following table.

| Situation | Threatening Response | Nonthreatening Response |
|---|---|---|
| You meet a guy for the first time. | "Hello." | "I am a nun." |
| You're on your first date. The guy asks you what your hopes for the future are. | "Well, I'd like to pursue my career for a while, and then get married and maybe have children." | "A vodka Collins." |
| You have a great time on the date, and the guy asks you if you'd like to go out again. | "Yes." | "Okay, but bear in mind that I have only three months to live." |
| The clergyperson asks you if you take this man to be your lawful wedded husband, for richer and poorer, in sickness and in health, etc., 'til death do you part. | "I do." | "Well, sure, but not *literally*." |

# 5

# Guy Problems

The Pain. The Anguish.
The Men's Room.

ONE OF THE biggest problems that guys have is that a lot of people—and here I am referring to women—think that guys don't *have* any problems.

"What problems can guys have?" women are always saying, just out of earshot. "Guys don't worry about relationships. They don't care whether the windows have any kind of window treatments. They can't see dirt or get pregnant. They're *supposed* to have facial hair. They can wear basically the same outfit for their entire lives—to work, dinner, church, the theater, parties, weddings, bar mitzvahs—and then they can be buried in it. All their socks are the same color. They can pee standing up."

Yes, to members of certain other genders the life of the guy looks pretty ideal. But beneath the placid surface of the average guy, there is raging inner turmoil and pain. The outside observer is not aware of this. Even the guy is usually not aware of this, especially if his mind is occupied with a pennant race.

But the turmoil, pain, etc., are there nonetheless. Because a guy must constantly deal with certain kinds of problems that only guys face, and that never get talked about on Oprah Winfrey[1] or Sally Jessy Raphael.[2] I'm talking about very serious problems, here; agonizing problems; extremely complex problems; terrible problems; problems so gut-wrenchingly problematical that it is difficult even for a trained professional writer such as myself to put them into words, because quite frankly I haven't figured out what they are yet. I'm just stalling for time here while I think them up.

Okay, I have one. A serious problem that guys face is:

## The Hardware-Store Problem

Picture yourself in this situation: You're a guy, and you've just walked into a hardware store, and you're

[1]Today: People Who Have Sex with Trees.
[2]Today: People Who Eat Their Children, *Then* Have Sex with Trees.

holding some kind of broken thing. This thing might be a "bearing." You're not sure, though; it could also be a "sprocket," a "gasket," or even a "volt." You just don't know. You've *never* really known what any of these things are, except that they are found inside the various mechanical objects that guys are supposed to understand, automatically, as though mechanical aptitude were a growth stage in male puberty. One day you wake up and discover that your armpits are sprouting little hairs; the next day you wake with the ability to repair a transmission.

*But this never happened to you.* This is your dirty little guy secret: You have *no clue* as to how mechanical things work. The last mechanical thing you ever did was in Wood Shop, when during a four-month attempt to make a bookshelf, you successfully nailed your shirt to a board. When you look at something mechanical, such as the internal workings of an automobile, or an appliance, or an airplane, or a toilet, all you see is a mass of random, dirty items, which you can identify only as "parts." And they all look like the *same* part. As far as you can tell, all mechanical devices are basically the same inside; you secretly believe that with only minor modifications, a Toyota could produce ice cubes, and a commode could play compact discs, and an Amana freezer could cruise at an altitude of thirty-seven thousand feet.

But of course you'd never tell anybody that you

feel this way, because you, like most guys, believe that all the *other* guys really understand how mechanical things work. And the hell of it is, some of them actually do. These are the guys—usually named "Steve"—whom you are forced to summon to your house when you suspect that you might have a serious mechanical problem.

Usually you try to ignore mechanical problems. Usually, in fact, you deny that they even exist, because you don't want to confront the fact that you are incapable of fixing anything. Over the years, especially since you got married, you've become highly skilled at pretending that things are not broken when they clearly are. Let's say your wife points out that the front door will not open, and her tone of voice clearly indicates that she thinks it should.

"Honey," you say, in the exasperated, slightly condescending voice that guys use when discussing mechanical things with their wives so as to disguise the fact that they are full of shit, "It's not *supposed* to open. This particular door is a type of security door that is supposed to, after you have had it for a certain number of years, just stay closed all the time."

Or say the kids tell you that the toaster bursts into flame when they push down the lever.

"Kids!" you say. "How many times do I have to tell you? That toaster is for *outdoor use only.*"

But some household mechanical problems simply cannot be ignored. Let's say one morning, while watching the kids extinguish their toast, you happen to glance into the living room, and you notice that it has fallen into your basement. Even *you* can't deny that this is a problem. To maintain your masculine dignity, you pretend that you're actually capable of dealing with this situation.

"Okay," you say to your wife, as you look down into the vast, gaping, rubble-strewn pit where your living room used to be. "I'll need some duct tape."

But you're not fooling anybody. Eventually you have to break down and call Steve.

Steve arrives in a truck. It's a big truck. Steve is a big guy. His forearms are bigger than your Barca-Lounger. He strides into your house (casually, on his way in, fixing the door that won't open) and spends a few minutes squinting at the problem in a knowledgeable manner. Then he calls you over.

"Mr. Barry," he says, "I want to show you something."

This is the part you hate. It's always bad when they want to show you something.

"Take a look at this," Steve says, pointing to a random house part. "You see this?"

You look at it and frown. You have no idea what particular part Steve is pointing at. It could be a "rafter." It could be a "drywall." It could be a "joist." It could be a "gable." It could be the steering wheel from the *Titanic*.

"Huh," you say, looking at it.

"Yup," says Steve. "You got a problem."

"What kind of problem?" you say, and Steve gives you a little sideways look, which tells you that, in his view, you are the stupidest homeowner he has ever met who was still able to walk erect. He can't *wait* to tell the gang all about you tonight when he goes to the Competent Guys' Tavern. Because this problem is spectacularly obvious to a guy like Steve. A guy like Steve can diagnose this kind of problem while under anesthesia. So there is a distinct tone of condescension in his voice, similar to the tone you used in explaining the security-door concept to your wife, when Steve explains to you exactly what the problem is, as simply and as clearly as he can.

"You got calcification in your pullet-beam header grommets," he says.

"I was afraid of that," you say.

"Yup," says Steve.

"Can it be fixed?" you ask.

"Well, *sure* it can be fixed," says Steve, who cannot believe what an idiot he is hooked up with here. "All you got to do is jack up your laminate bolts and winch in a three-sixteenths catheter truncheon."

When Steve says "you," of course, he does not mean

"you." The only tool *you* own is a set of toenail clippers.[3] Whereas Steve has a wide assortment of both jacks and winches. Steve's *children* play with jacks and winches. Steve has every kind of tool he'll ever need for anything, right in his truck. If the world economy ever collapses, and mankind regresses to a primitive state, guys like Steve will be living in sturdy, safe shelters that they built with their own hands, eating food that they grew or caught. Whereas guys like you will be passing through the digestive systems of wolves.

So Steve, sweating the sweat of honest labor, starts jacking and winching your house, and you go off to begin *your* work day, during which the most challenging physical task you will be called upon to perform is chewing.

Eventually Steve fixes your house, and you write him a large check, and he heads off to his next job. But you notice that he continues to be a topic of interest among the members of your family.

"I saw Steve today," your wife will say. "He was lifting Audrey Pootermaker's car out of a ditch."

"With a winch?" you ask.

"No," says your wife, and you definitely detect a certain dreaminess in her voice. "He was just *lifting* it."

"*Wow!*" says your son, who then resumes playing with the miniature submarine—powered by a tiny but

---

[3]And you, as a result, are minus one toe.

fully functional nuclear reactor—that Steve made for him out of empty Sprite cans.

Naturally this bothers you. You wonder, What's the big deal? Sure, Steve can do a lot of stuff, but could he do some of the things *you* know how to do? Could he analyze a financial spreadsheet, for example? Could he make a *four-way conference call*? Hah! You'd like to see Steve try *that*.

But you know you're only fooling yourself. You really wish you had some mechanical competence. Finally you decide that you are by gosh going to do something about it. You go to the Sears tool department to equip yourself:

SALESPERSON: May I help you?

YOU: Yes. I'd like to buy a tool.

SALESPERSON: What kind?

YOU: Not too heavy.

You come home with a fifty-three-piece socket-wrench set in a neat little carrying case. Sometimes, when nobody else is around, you open it up, take out one of the little socket things and click it onto the end of the long handle thing. Then you prowl around the house, squinting knowledgeably at mechanical objects and looking alert, in case you happen across something that needs to be wrenched. You feel you are ready. All you need is a break.

And then, one Saturday morning, you get your big chance. . . .

"Dear," your wife says, "I think there's a problem with the water heater."

"What kind of problem?" you ask in what is, for you, a pretty deep voice.

"The kind of problem where we need to call Steve," says your wife.

"No need for that," you say, in the same fairly deep voice. And then with a smooth, practiced motion, you grab the handle of your socket-wrench-kit case. And then, with an easy physical grace that you would not have thought yourself capable of, you crouch down on the floor to pick up the fifty-three pieces, which have fallen out because you forgot to latch the case.

With a look of grim determination, you march into the garage. There, after spending several minutes sizing up the situation and carefully analyzing the physical evidence, you are able to put your finger on the problem: *The water heater is located in the basement.*

So you march down there, and sure enough, something is wrong with the water heater, which is dribbling water onto the floor and making a loud groaning noise. You instantly recognize these as classic mechanical symptoms, which can only mean one thing. That's right: The water heater is pregnant! It's about to have a baby water heater! You'll need hot water, and plenty of it!

No, you think; get a grip on yourself. You open your socket-wrench case, carefully select a socket thing at random, and place it on the handle thing. Your wife has come downstairs to watch you. You approach the water heater carefully, on the balls of your feet, looking for an opening, hoping that it will let its guard down for a second so you can get in there and fix it. You notice a little box on the side of the heater, with wires coming out; this looks like a vulnerable area. You probe it with your wrench. Nothing happens. You probe it a little harder. Nothing happens. You realize that this is probably the type of box that is designed to be struck with great force, so you whack it with the wrench handle. The cover comes off. Your wife, making a noise not unlike the one the water heater is making, goes back upstairs.

Inside the box, just as you suspected, you find: parts. Now you're getting somewhere! Using the wrench handle, you probe around among the parts, looking for some sign of trouble, such as a part holding up a small hand-lettered sign that says HELP ME. Suddenly you see a spark, and you hear a *pop,* and one of the parts falls onto the floor. At that same moment, *the water heater stops groaning.* Hurrah!

On the other hand, all the lights have gone off. Also you can smell smoke. But there's an old do-it-yourselfer saying: "You can't make an omelette without breaking eggs and cutting off the electrical power and possibly setting fire to your home."

You are not worried, however. You figure all you

have to do now, to finish the job, is to find the fallen part—which was obviously the root of the problem—and go get a new one at the hardware store. So you root around on your hands and knees in the darkness and dampness until you find the part. At least you *think* it's the part. It could also be something hard that was regurgitated long ago by the dog. Whatever it is, it will have to do, because you are not particularly comfortable in the darkened basement environment. You have seen spiders down here the size of bus tires. Next time you will carry a larger socket wrench.

And so, clutching the part, you go upstairs, noting—here is an amazing coincidence—that the power is off up here, too. Also it seems a little smoky. You'll have to look into this, once you've straightened out the water-heater thing.

"I'm going to the hardware store," you tell your wife, who is sitting at the kitchen table, head down, whimpering. That's the thing about women: They get emotional over a little thing like a broken water heater, and that's why they can't be relied upon to take action and *deal* with a situation.

And thus we come back to our opening scene: You, a lone guy, arrive at the hardware store, holding a broken part that you don't know the name of. You wander through the store aisles, looking for a part that might be the same as the one you have. Around you, this Saturday morning, are perhaps a dozen other guys. Each one of them, like you, is in the middle of a some kind of home-repair project that has gone past the Point of No Return—the guy has taken something apart and removed some critical part, and even if the part wasn't broken *before,* it certainly is *now,* and unless the guy can find one like it, he is in serious homeowner trouble.

So you guys are wandering the aisles, frowning intently at the hardware store's thousands of items, comparing them with the parts in your hands, looking for a match. And of course all of you will fail. The hardware store *never* has the part you're looking for. This is the fundamental law of guy do-it-yourselfing. Not only does the hardware store not have your part; *nobody* has your part. It's the only part of its kind in the entire world. When it was made, the original manufacturer destroyed all the plans and executed the workers involved, so as to ensure that this part could never be reproduced.

But for a while you continue your fruitless search. You go from hardware store to home center, still carrying your part. You become good friends with other guys who are also on parts quests. Sometimes you all exchange parts, just so everybody will have something new to look for. Eventually some of the guys wander off to look for their parts in other states, maybe other countries. Some of them apply for positions in NASA, in hopes of someday searching for their parts in other galaxies.

But you're more of a realist, and eventually you realize that you're going to have to return to your dark, smoky house, to confront your failure, and apologize to your wife, and see how your children are doing, and—above all—get some clean underwear. And so one day you swallow your pride and go home. And there, sitting in your driveway, a massive, throbbing presence, is: Steve's truck.

And the pain you feel at that moment is something that no woman could ever understand.

## The Public-Rest Room Problem

This is a problem that guys face when they go into a public rest room. When women go into a rest room, they have the privacy of stalls, but guys have to do it while standing pretty much out in the open, sometimes with many other guys standing around.

This can be tricky, because peeing is very much associated, in guys' minds, with masculinity. Consider the behavior of guy dogs, who spend their lives in a ceaseless quest to establish their masculine dominance by peeing on everything in the entire world. Scientists believe that the reason dogs howl at the moon is because they (the dogs) (also some of the scientists) are upset that they can't get up there and pee on it.

As noted, I own two dogs: a large main dog named

Earnest, and a small emergency backup dog named Zippy. Earnest, a large female, pees only when she has to pee. Zippy, a tiny fluffy male, basically never stops peeing. He is like a small walking wad of cotton with urine constantly dribbling out of it. Sometimes he encounters the next-door neighbors' dog, Prince, and the two of them engage in a pee-fest. They'll sniff each other for a moment, rush off in a purposeful manner to squirt various bushes, then rush back together to sniff each other some more, then rush to the bushes again, back and forth, a pair of leaking, low-IQ testosterone tornadoes, each one firmly convinced that he is the biggest, baddest stud on the planet.

My point is that peeing has significance for guys that goes way beyond the mere elimination of bodily fluids. It is an important territorial statement. This is why, every time a guy enters a public rest room, he must confront a critical guy problem; namely: Which urinal should he use? His goal is to avoid, at all costs, peeing right next to another guy, because they would be infringing on each other's territories.

So in the ideal guy rest room, the urinals would be located a minimum of fifty feet apart. Unfortunately, in the real world, they're right next to each other, which means the guy often must make split-second strategic urinal decisions. To illustrate this process, let's imagine a public rest room in an airport. Let's assume the rest room has a row of five urinals, which are represented as rectangles is the following scientific diagram:

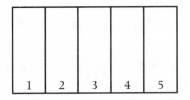

Let's further assume that nobody is in the room when Guy A walks in. He is almost always going to choose one of the end urinals—either no. 1 or no. 5—because he knows this will put him as far as possible from the next guy who comes along. Let's say Guy A chooses urinal no. 5, which means our situation is now this:

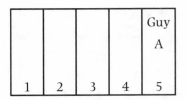

When Guy B walks in, he will *always* take no. 1. He would never, ever, in a billion years, take no. 4. To do such a thing would cause Guy A to become alarmed to the point where he might zip up his fly so fast that he risks wetting his pants and possibly even injuring his manhood, rather than remain there. But Guy B will always take the far urinal; he may be a decent, secure, open-minded, nonjudgmental person with absolutely no prejudice whatsoever toward gay people, but he nevertheless would rather poke both of his eyeballs out than have Guy A think that he *is* one. So he will go to the other end. If the line of urinals were a mile long, Guy B might very well choose to hike the entire distance, even if this meant he would miss his plane.

So now the situation is this:

| Guy B | | | | Guy A |
|---|---|---|---|---|
| 1 | 2 | 3 | 4 | 5 |

When Guy C comes in, he will clearly choose urinal no. 3. He is not crazy about it, but he still has a one-urinal buffer on each side:

| Guy B | Buffer Urinal | Guy C | Buffer Urinal | Guy A |
|---|---|---|---|---|
| 1 | 2 | 3 | 4 | 5 |

But now in comes Guy D, and *he* has a real guy problem, because whatever urinal he picks, he'll be right next to two other guys. This is very upsetting. Some guys in this situation will choose to pee in an enclosed stall, or wait until there's a buffered urinal available, or go way off to the side and pee against the wall, as follows:

| Guy B | | Guy C | | Guy A | Guy D |
|---|---|---|---|---|---|
| 1 | 2 | 3 | 4 | 5 | |

If Guy D *does* go to one of the available urinals—say no. 2—he and guys B and C will all stand rigid, staring intently straight ahead, as though the wall tiles were inscribed with a secret formula for turning Grape Nuts into platinum. DEATH BEFORE EYE CONTACT, that is the motto of a guy at a public urinal.

I realize that you women out there think I'm making all this up. But ask the guy in your life to read this section, and I bet he'll nod in recognition. He's been there, and he knows the behavior I'm describing. But he has never felt comfortable about discussing this subject with you, because this is an extremely sensitive area for him. Also he knows it's stupid. Although it doesn't hold a candle in that department to an even bigger kind of guy problem—possibly the biggest guy problem of all:

## Sports Anguish

Guys are very vulnerable to this. Because guys care about sports teams. I'm not talking about simply rooting; I'm talking about a *relationship* that guys develop, a *commitment* to a sports team that guys take way more seriously than, for example, wedding vows.

When a guy gets married, he might *say* that it's for richer or poorer, until death do them part, etc., but he knows, somewhere in the deep[4] recesses of his mind, that something could come up to make him change his mind, possibly even during the reception. Whereas the bond he forms with a sports team is *permanent.*

You may feel that there is something twisted about the values of a guy who can be more committed to a bunch of transient athletes—none of whom he really knows, and none of whom care about him—than he is to his own wife. But you have to consider the larger picture, from the guy's point of view: His wife may be a warm, loving, and loyal person, but *there is no way she will ever make the play-offs.* Not even if she really works out and bulks up during the off-season. Whereas there is always a chance that, if the guy remains faithful, his team eventually will not only make the play-offs, but also even win the championship.[5]

But—every guy secretly believes this—the team can succeed *only if he really cares about it,* really devotes himself exclusively to it night and day, even if this means he must neglect his family and his career and

[4]About three quarters of an inch, for most guys.
[5]Unless, of course, the team is the Boston Red Sox.

the threat of global warming. If he does this, he can make a difference; he can be a *part* of the winning effort; he can contribute to the victory in every way that the athletes themselves do, except in those ways that involve actually doing something athletic.

I have experienced this firsthand. Back when I lived in Philadelphia, I shared season tickets to the Philadelphia 76ers professional basketball team with a friend of mine named Buzz Burger. These were great seats, right behind the visitors' bench. We could listen to everything the opposing coach said, and offer helpful suggestions and words of encouragement. Sometimes we were so encouraging that the opposing coach would yell helpful suggestions rhyming with "duck shoe" back at us, causing the dedicated fans around us to give us high-five congratulatory handshakes.

But our main function, and we took it very seriously, was to ensure that the 76ers won. We did this by being deeply concerned about them, to the point of derangement. If you were to go back and carefully analyze videotapes of certain critical parts of certain critical games, you would see faint but definitely visible Concern Rays shooting out of Buzz's and my heads onto the basketball court, affecting the course of the game.

The ultimate instance of this occurred in a game during the 1985–86 season, when the 76ers were playing the Boston Celtics. This game remains one of the high points of my life. It was a game that, as a human achievement, ranks right up there with penicillin.

You should understand that, as a longtime 76ers fan, I hated the Celtics. Not in the way I hate, for example, Hitler, but more often.

In this game, the 76ers did not have their center, Moses Malone, who was a major world rebounding power and a large enough individual that he, personally, should have been represented by at least three members of Congress. Without him in there, the 76ers were struggling, and Boston led most of the way. It looked like the Celtics would win easily, which was bad enough; what made it worse was that there were three Boston fans sitting right behind us, and of course they were typical Boston fans, by which I mean they accounted for two thirds of the known world supply of smug. They weren't so much rooting as they were smirking loudly, right in our ears, the whole game, saying it was a joke, no contest, and that Julius Erving, the 76ers' captain, was over the hill. Which he was, but these people had no right to say so. Because Julius Erving was, and still is, a fine individual, and if the voters would have the common sense to elect him president, instead of the goobers we keep putting in there, this nation would be a lot better off than it is now.

So anyway, despite not having Malone, the 76ers managed to hang in the game, and with less than thirty seconds left they had pulled within two points. That was the good news. The bad news was that Larry Bird, the Celtic legend, was going to shoot two foul shots.

People wonder, sometimes, how come white people don't play basketball as well as black people. The answer, I believe, is that for some reason Nature decided to concentrate all of the natural basketball ability for the entire white race for the past fifty years into Larry Bird.

So most people in the crowd figured Bird was going to make these shots and put the game out of reach. The three smirking Beantown fans behind me just *knew* it. And you could tell that Larry Bird knew it, too, as he stepped up to the foul line, bounced the ball, and cocked his arm to shoot.

I read an article once stating that down in Central America, they take sports a little too seriously in the sense that they routinely kill each other over soccer. (For the record, I think this is overreacting, unless of course once again we are talking about the play-offs.)

So anyway, there was this big match once where El Salvador beat Honduras, or the other way around, and the next day one of the newspapers in the winning country claimed that the foot of Jesus had actually come down from heaven several times and deflected shots from the winning team's goal. There was an actual drawing of this in the newspaper.

Now, you may laugh at this, but I do not. Because a very similar thing happened in the 76ers–Celtics game, except that it was not the foot of Jesus (although He might have helped). It was Concern Rays emanating from Buzz and me at a level of intensity that we had never before achieved. These rays shot laserlike from our foreheads, intercepted the ball at the height of its arc, and *caused Larry Bird to miss twice*.

I am not seeking praise here. I am merely stating a fact.

And now the 76ers had the ball. They tried to run a play but they screwed up, and wound up with Charles Barkley, who is six feet, six inches tall and slightly greater in width, in a jump-ball situation against the Celtics' Kevin McHale, who is six-ten. And there were three seconds left. And the crowd was on its feet, making more noise than all Space Shuttle launches combined.

And here is what happened: *Barkley wins the tap.* And the ball goes to Julius Erving, the old over-the-hill Doctor J, who is guarded by Danny Ainge, the whiny little weenie cheap-shot-specialist guard, and—there is one second on the clock now—Erving *launches a three-point shot.*

Buzz and I know we can help this shot. But—this is the kind of self-sacrificing fans we are—we want Doctor J to have the glory. So we leave his shot alone, and it arcs upward over Ainge's hand, and over all the Celtics' heads, even Larry Bird's, and then it arcs downward downward downward and

## *SWISH*

it goes clean through. The buzzer sounds. The game is over. The Sixers win. The public-address system, cranked up loud enough to be heard clearly in Guam, starts playing the Isley Brothers' version of *Shout.* And Buzz and I, moving smoothly, like well-trained dancers who have had several beers apiece, leap to our feet, whirl to face the Boston fans behind us, and cup our hands to our ears, indicating by this gesture our concern over the fact that, for the first time all game, *we don't hear them saying anything.*

And of course they have nothing to say.

My point is, a guy can get *involved* with a team. This can enable the guy to experience wonderful, magical moments, like the one I just described. But it also makes the guy vulnerable—yes, *vulnerable*—to a kind of emotional distress that, frankly, many women cannot imagine.

Tune in to any radio sports-talk show and you'll get an idea of what I'm talking about. You'll hear human misery of a magnitude rarely found outside of intensive-care units. You'll hear guys who rarely show their emotions, guys who don't cry at funerals, guys who are reluctant to openly hug their own children—you'll hear these guys coming close to tears over sports events that may have occurred *years* ago. (If you want to see raw pain, just walk up to any guy Red Sox fan and say: "How about that Bill Buckner error in the 1986 World Series?" Go ahead! Ask him! It's fun!)

As I write these words, in the summer of 1993, in Miami, Florida, I'm listening to a sports-talk radio show on which the callers—all of them guys—are extremely upset about the Dave Magadan trade. It's all they want to talk about.

For those of you who do not follow world events, I should explain that Dave Magadan was a player for the Florida Marlins, who traded him to Seattle. A lot of guys down here believe that this trade was a mistake, that the Marlins should have traded a player named Orestes Destrade instead. And so these guys call the talk shows, night and day, to vent their feelings. The thing is, the Magadan trade took place *three weeks ago.* I seriously doubt that even Magadan is still talking about it.

But that doesn't matter to these guys. Nor does it matter that they don't personally know either Magadan or Destrade, or that this trade will have no observable impact on their lives. What matters is that they *care,* which is why they cannot stop themselves from picking away endlessly at this particular emotional scab:

SPORTS-TALK-SHOW HOST: You're on the air.

CALLER: I am *really* upset about this Magadan trade. I think it sucks. I can't *believe* they . . .

HOST: Hold it! I've just been handed a news bulletin! It says that the Turkey Point nuclear generating plant has blown up, and South Florida is being covered by a giant radioactive cloud!

CALLER: I mean, we're talking about a guy who was a *lifetime three-hundred hitter.*

Of course I'm making up the preceding dialogue. It's unrealistic in the sense that (a) the Turkey Point nuclear plant did *not* blow up, and (b) even if it did, the host would never interrupt the show with such a frivolous topic so soon after a major roster move.

Because he is also a guy.

In this chapter, I have presented a few of the unique problems that guys must face each day. Rest assured that guys have plenty of other problems, and they can be just as devastating and traumatic. Ear hair springs to mind. But I'm not going to dwell on these problems, because part of the Guy Code is to be tough, to not complain, to bear up silently under hardships that would bring a lesser gender to its knees.

Also my fingers are tired.

# 6

# Special Medical Concerns of the Guy, or: "It's Just a Sprain"

THE GUY BODY is unlike the female body. And I am not talking here about the obvious peaks and valleys. I am talking about a unique guy physical problem, a severe genetic handicap that poses a grave risk to the health of the guy body; namely, it is under the control of the guy mind.

The guy mind does not believe in medical care. Guys will generally not seek medical treatment, for themselves or for others, except in certain clear-cut situations, such as decapitation. And even then, guys are not going to be 100 percent certain. "Let's put his head back on with duct tape and see if he can play a couple more innings," is the prevailing guy attitude.

There is a reason for this. If you are a guy, you have learned, the hard way, that when you get involved in a medical situation, even as a bystander, there is always a chance that a medical professional will suddenly, without warning, put on a rubber glove and stick his hand up your butt, looking for your prostate. Most guys have no idea what a "prostate" is, but they're pretty sure that if they had one up their butt, they'd already know about it.

So guys are suspicious of medical care. I will illustrate this attitude with a true anecdote involving a guy I know named Ted Shields. I met Ted through an outfit that he cofounded, along with a co-guy named Pat Monahan:

The World Famous Lawn Rangers Precision Lawnmower Drill Team of Arcola, Illinois.

Arcola (slogan: "Amazing Arcola") is a small town in central Illinois (slogan: "You Bet It's Flat"). At one time Arcola was a major producer of broom corn, which is a type of corn used to make brooms.[1] The town is still an important player in the broom-manufacturing industry and boasts one of the world's largest collections of antique brooms and brushes. It also has

[1]Duh.

one of the world's largest rocking chairs, as well as an establishment called the French Embassy, which is the world's only combination gourmet French restaurant and bowling alley. I am not making this up.

Every year in September, Arcola holds a Broom Corn Festival featuring a parade, and one of the most popular units in this parade is the world-famous Lawn Rangers, who march down the street pushing customized lawnmowers,[2] carrying brooms, and performing precision broom-and-lawnmower marching maneuvers. The members are mostly pillars of the community who believe that it is possible to have a good time and yet do absolutely nothing useful for society.

I was deeply honored when I was invited to join the Rangers a few years back. It is not easy to belong to this exclusive unit: Membership is strictly limited to anybody who shows up on parade day at Ted Shields's garage. This is where Ranger Orientation is held. Ranger Orientation consists of:

(1) **Mental Preparation**, by which I mean drinking beer;[3]

(2) the **Business Meeting**, which consists of activities too juvenile to mention even in this book, except to say that it involves, among other things, a man climbing up a ladder and, using props, presenting a dramatic

[2]One of them, for example, has a toilet on it.
[3]The Rangers continue to engage in Mental Preparation well after the parade is over. "You can't be too prepared" is one of their mottoes.

rendition of a song, while the Rangers attempt to guess the title, which is not difficult because the song always involves the word "moon";[4] and

(3) **Rookie Camp**, which is where first-time Rangers, under the gentle yet firm guidance of seasoned veterans (*"Listen up, you gravy-sucking pigs!"*) learn the Rangers' precision marching maneuvers,[5] which consist of

a. "Walk the Dog," which is when you hold your broom in the air with one hand and turn your lawnmower in a 360-degree circle with the other, and

b. "Cross and Toss," which is when the two marching columns of Rangers switch sides; then toss their brooms in the air to each other; then try to catch the brooms; then, a lot of the time, miss.

Often the rookies must spend as long as two minutes in the grueling central-Illinois sun before they can perform these routines at the level of precision for which the Rangers are known.

Once Rookie Camp is complete, the Rangers form approximately two columns and march in the parade. If you have never been there, it is difficult for me to explain to you the feeling of electricity in the air as the Rangers, wearing their traditional uniforms of cowboy-style hats and Halloween-style masks to preserve their secret identities, wheel their mowers down the

---

[4]The props for "Moon Over Miami" involved two coconuts and a banana.
[5]Do not try these maneuvers at home.

main parade route; and the Column Leaders—who carry long-handled toilet plungers to denote their rank—give the "Brooms Up!" command in preparation for a precision maneuver; and fifty Rangers, like a well-engineered machine, simultaneously do approximately forty-five different things. All I can say is, if you are watching us, you had better have a strong bladder.

I realize that I have gotten away from the actual chapter topic, which is guy medical concerns, but I felt I needed to get a plug into this book for the Lawn Rangers, an outfit that truly epitomizes the concept of Guyness. My feeling is that if more guys would join mellow, purposeless, and semi-dysfunctional organizations such as the Lawn Rangers, then there would be a lot fewer guys getting involved in aggressive, venal, destructive, and frequently criminal organizations such as the U.S. Congress.

But my immediate anecdote concerns Ranger co-founder Ted Shields, who was with some other Rangers on a fishing trip off the coast of Louisiana when he came down wrong on his ankle and broke it. Naturally he told everybody it was just a sprain. Guys always say it's "just a sprain," because this way they can avoid falling into the clutches of medical care. A guy could have one major limb lying on the ground a full ten feet from the rest of his body, and he'd claim it was "just a sprain."

So although Ted's ankle was painful and swelling

rapidly and turning some nonstandard colors, Ted chose to remain on the boat and treat the injury himself.

"Fortunately," he recalls, "we had beer."

Following standard Red Cross procedure, Ted removed a number of cans from the cooler to make room in the ice for his foot.

"This meant we had to drink the beers immediately, lest they become warm," he recalls. "But you do what you have to do."

The Rangers fished for the remainder of the day— Ted fished with his foot in the cooler—then returned to land, where, that evening, knowing that they had an injured man and not wanting to take any chances, they all went dancing.

"My foot was hurting pretty bad," Ted recalls, "but I was one of the few Rangers who did not fall down that night."

The next day they returned to Arcola, where Ted's wife, Joyce, a keen observer, observed that (a) he could barely walk, and (b) one of his legs had become much larger than the other; in fact, larger than some entire persons.

"It was a Pillsbury Doughboy leg," is how Joyce describes it.

"It's just a sprain," is what Ted told her.

Nevertheless Joyce insisted on taking him to the hospital, where she had to fill out all the medical forms, because Ted was busy explaining to the hospital personnel that he didn't really need treatment.

"His ankle was *grotesque*," Joyce recalls. "People were staring at it, and I was trying to get these papers filled out, and Ted was leaning over my shoulder and saying 'It's just a sprain.' "

A number of weeks later, Ted got out of his cast, in time to march in the Broom Corn Parade. So all's well that ends well. But my point is that, if there is a guy in your life, and you want him to get decent medical care, you cannot rely on him or Hillary Clinton to be responsible for it. You have to use a technique that was perfected by wildlife officials for use with bears and rhinoceroses, namely: tranquilizer darts. This is the only way you can be sure of getting a guy to a medical-care facility in a timely manner if he has, for example, injured himself during a touch-football game, and you have pointed out that there are bones sticking from his body, plus some aortal bleeding, but he is claiming that this condition will probably go away on its own. In this case you should fire a dart or two into his body, let him stagger around for a few more plays until he collapses, then strap him to the trunk of the car and take him to the hospital. And when you get him there, be sure to tell the doctors that, in addition to his obvious injuries . . . he has been complaining about his prostate.

He deserves it.

**Guy Medical Conditions**

Thus far we have been discussing the basic guy attitude toward medical care, which may be summarized as follows: stupid. But we also need to discuss specific medical conditions that guys are prone to, such as:

Guy Vision

This is a condition that guys have that makes them unable to see certain types of details. Notice I say "certain types." There are *some* details that guys can see extremely well. For example, a guy at a baseball game can see with perfect clarity that the umpire has made a totally wrong and possibly criminal call on a close play at home plate. A guy can see this type of detail even though he has had four beers and is several hundred feet from the actual play; some guys can see this type of detail perfectly *even if they were in the men's room when the play occurred.*

Also guys can see naked female breasts at unbelievable distances. If there is a breast around, a guy will see it. And once he sees it, he is pretty much unable to stop looking at it, no matter what else is going on (see the section in chapter 2 on Lust-Induced Brain Freeze). Not long ago, I was at Miami Beach, having brunch with a coeducational group, and after we ate we decided to walk on the beach. It was a beautiful sunny day, and we were talking, and suddenly the three guys spotted two naked breasts, which, as it happened, belonged to a woman who was lying on a towel. Now, a lot of women sunbathe in a topless manner on Miami Beach. They're very casual about it, and I try to *act* casual about it, but in fact it never ceases to astound me that this is happening. When I was an adolescent, the only reliable source of breast visuals was *National Geographic*, a magazine then devoted, as far as I could tell, to doing feature articles on every primitive tribe in the world in which the women went around topless. When I was in junior high school, my friends and I were *extremely* interested in these articles, specifically the photographs that had captions like "A young woman of the Mbonga tribe prepares supper using primitive implements." We would spend long periods of time staring at the young woman's implements, and we'd wonder how come we'd had the incredibly bad luck of being born in the one society in the entire world (judging from *National Geographic*) wherein women wore a lot of clothes. If there had been a beach near us where women sunbathed topless, we would have *lived* there, surviving by eating jellyfish.

So anyway, when we three guys noticed the sunbathing woman, we immediately flashed each other, via subtle covert glances, the Urgent Code Red Priority One Naked Breast Alert signal. We tried to look as unconcerned as possible—A topless woman! Big deal!—

and we continued chatting with the women, appearing to be interested in the conversation, but in fact our bodies were dividing up our available brainpower as follows:

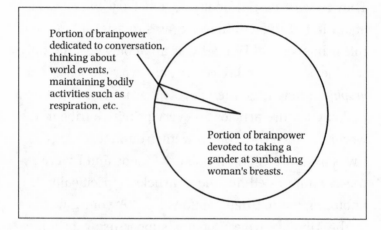

Portion of brainpower dedicated to conversation, thinking about world events, maintaining bodily activities such as respiration, etc.

Portion of brainpower devoted to taking a gander at sunbathing woman's breasts.

My point is that guys *are* capable of tremendous visual concentration. Unfortunately, they have no say in the decision as to what their eyeballs choose to concentrate *on*, which means that they often miss certain subtle details, such as what their wives look like. Take the case of a couple I know named (really) Steele and Bobette Reeder. One time Bobette was getting ready to substantially change her hairstyle, and, in a gesture of compassion, she decided to alert Steele.

"Steele," she said, "you never notice when I change my hair, so this time I'm telling you ahead of time: I'm going to get a new hairstyle today. It's going to look completely different."

So that evening, when Steele got home from work, he immediately started raving about how nice Bobette's hair looked, how much better he liked it, etc. He was so excited about her new hairstyle that she had to interrupt him to say: "Steele, they canceled my appointment."

Even when guys *do* notice women's hair, they can get in trouble. Here is part of a letter I got from a guy named John Maines, describing an incident involving a woman he was seeing named Shawn:

> Once I drove my car into Georgetown here in D.C. to pick her up after she had gotten a "perm." I was all flustered because the traffic was very heavy and I had gotten lost on the way in and was late getting to the street corner where I was supposed to pick her up.
>
> Shawn got into the car, her long hair all kinked up. It looked good, but I was still concentrating on driving. After a minute, she said, "You don't like it, do you?"
>
> "Not at all," I replied, staring ahead, hands firmly gripped on the wheel. "I bet it will take a half an hour just to get three blocks."
>
> Anyway, today Shawn and I are what she calls "best friends" (every guy knows what that means, sex-wise).

Many guys also have a problem seeing details of their own personal selves. This is why there are guys walking around, convinced that they are the most irresistible stud muffins on the continent, while wearing shirts that stop about three inches above their belts, thus allowing maybe twenty-five pounds of hairy, pasty, belly-buttoned flab to thrust itself out, looking like a bloated mutant one-eyed albino walrus trying to escape from their pants. This is why some guys honestly believe they can comb their remaining hair in a realistic, even attractive manner over bald spots the size of American Samoa.

A lot of guys can't see dirt. This is why they're so bad at cleaning chores around the house. Partly, of course, this is because they have learned that if they do a bad enough job, they will no longer be *asked* to do cleaning chores around the house, but mainly it's because dirt is flat invisible to them. They are capable of "cleaning" a bathroom in such a way that, when they are done, it still contains active mildew colonies capable of capturing and eating a small dog.

A variation of this is Floor Blindness. My son, Rob, has this. Ordinarily he has eyes like an eagle's: He can read Stephen King books in total darkness, see brownies through a solid kitchen-cabinet door, and spot a Burger King sign seventeen miles away. But he *cannot* see things that are on the floor, particularly if they are his things. I'll say to him, "Rob, I want you to pick up your room," and he'll say, in an annoyed voice, "I already did," and I'll go into his room to inspect the floor, and *I can't even see it.* It is *completely* covered with layers and layers of Rob's stuff. It is entirely possible that Jimmy Hoffa is buried under there somewhere. I could not swear, in a court of law, that he *has* a floor.

But as much of a problem as Guy Vision is, it is not nearly as serious as a related guy medical condition, namely:

## Guy Memory Lapses

The basic problem here is that guys, as I have noted, devote so much of their brains to remembering vital facts such as who was named MVP of the 1978 Super Bowl that they cannot always remember minor details, such as that they have left an infant on the roof of a car.

You think I'm exaggerating, but I'm not. According to a 1992 *Boston Globe* article that was sent to me by various alert readers, a guy in Massachusetts did this on *Mother's Day.* He had his two children with him, and he was loading them into his car, and he *did*—give him credit—remember to strap his twenty-month-old daughter into the car. But the amount of concentration required for a guy to remember this type of child-care detail can put a lot of strain on his mental equipment, so he went into acute Guy Memory Lapse and forgot that he had placed a car seat containing his three-month-old son on the roof of the car. As he accelerated onto Interstate 290, he sensed that something was wrong when, according to the *Globe,* "he heard a scraping sound on the roof of the car."

(This is classic guy behavior: He *doesn't* notice that

he has only 50 percent of his total children inside the car with him, but he *does* notice that his car is making a funny sound.)

Anyway, the car was going about fifty miles per hour when the car seat containing the three-month-old boy sailed off the roof and landed on Interstate 290, where—this is strong evidence that God is a guy—the seat skidded safely to a stop, with the boy unhurt. So the story has a happy ending, except of course that this particular guy had to tell his wife what happened *(Happy Mother's Day!)*. I bet she rolled her eyeballs into the next *state*.

Perhaps you are saying: "Dave, aren't you being unfair? Aren't you using purely anecdotal evidence to reinforce an unfortunate gender stereotype about men? Isn't it entirely possible that a *woman* could leave her child on the car roof and drive off?"

No.

Nor do I think it is likely that anybody other than a guy could have been responsible for another Adventure in Motoring that was reported in 1992 by the Scripps-Howard News Service. This involved a Colorado guy who pulled his van out of a gas station near Washington, Pennsylvania, and drove through West Virginia and part of Ohio without noticing that his wife, the mother of two children, was still back at the gas station in Pennsylvania. The guy assumed she was sleeping in the back of their van. He made it almost to Columbus, Ohio, where he pulled over and—still not noticing anything unusual—decided to take a nap. Only after waking up an hour and a half later did he realize that his wife was not, technically, in the van with him. At this point he turned around and began driving frantically back east on Route 70, getting as far as Wheeling, West Virginia, where he hit a deer. The accident damaged his van, so he walked to a truck stop, where he was reunited with his wife, who had been transported westward by helpful police.

Guess what day this happened on.

That's right: *Mother's Day.* I am still not making this up.

I'll give you one more clinical case history of Guy Memory Lapse; this was reported in the police roundup section of *The Mining Journal* of Marquette, Michigan, and sent to me by alert readers Tina and Dan McFaddin. It concerns a couple who were driving in a rural area, devoid of rest stops, when nature called. The item begins as follows:

> NEGAUNEE—A Wisconsin woman suffered broken ribs when her husband accidentally backed over her in their pickup truck Monday night while she was urinating.

Miraculously, this incident did *not* occur on Mother's Day. And if this woman has any sense, when Mother's

Day *does* roll around, she will barricade herself in a bomb shelter until it's over.

We see from these examples that Guy Memory Lapse is mainly hazardous to other people. But there are certain uniquely guy medical situations that are hazardous only to the guy, the scariest of which involves:

## Threats to the Guy Privates

I am not suggesting here that only guys have privates. I realize that women also have privates, and plenty of them. But their privates are a lot more *private*. They are tucked safely away in various vaults of the female body; whereas the guy privates—which contain not only half of the guy's nerve endings, but also a good 83 percent of his motivation—are, because of an incredibly stupid design flaw, hanging right out in the open in an absurdly vulnerable manner,[6] like Harold Lloyd dangling from the face of the giant clock, waiting for disaster to strike.

Almost every guy has, at one time or another, been traumatically whacked in the personal region by a baseball or a bicycle bar or a knee or something, and this is the kind of thing a guy remembers for a *long* time. I can still vividly recall an incident in the fall of 1960, when a lot of us kids were let out of junior high

---

[6]Further evidence that Mother Nature is a woman.

school to see a big Republican campaign rally, featuring President Eisenhower, at the Westchester County (N.Y.) airport. There was a huge crowd, and my friend Emil Sommer and I were taking turns sitting on each other's shoulders in an effort to see better. Just as the presidential party was getting close, I slipped off my perch in such a way as to severely pound my personals[7] on Emil's elbow on the way down. I could probably have hurt myself worse, but only if I had used power tools.

So I was doubled over in extreme discomfort amidst several thousand cheering Westchester County Republicans shouting "There he is! There he is!" And I looked up, and there, briefly, through the throng, and through the reddish haze of my pain, I could see the smiling moonlike face and spasmodically waving arms of: Dick Nixon.

It was not, technically, his fault, but I was never able to look at him again without considerable discomfort.

But that incident was nothing, compared with what happened to a guy in Singapore in August of 1993. I quote here from a news account in *The Singapore Straits Times*:

> A former national shotput and discus champion was bitten on his testicles yesterday by a python hiding in a toilet bowl he was sitting on.

[7]Or, as the Mexicans say, "crunched my *cojones*."

*The Singapore Straits Times*—which covered this story the way *The New York Times* covers tension in the Middle East—dutifully noted that pythons have a "particularly nasty" bite because they have "rows of inward-curving, needle-sharp teeth." After the victim—whose name (I am *still* not making this up) is Fok Keng Choy—was stitched up[8] at the hospital, *The Singapore Straits Times* asked him about the pain, and he said eloquently: "Words could not describe it."

It took four men to pull the python out of the toilet bowl. The *Times* noted that a woman had used the very same toilet just forty-five minutes before Mr. Fok did, "but nothing happened," which just proves the point I am making here about the extreme guy vulnerability resulting from the Dangle Syndrome.

Another incidence of a penis being chomped on by irate wildlife was reported in September 1992 by the British newspaper *The Sun,* which stated that a carpenter sat down on a portable toilet at a building site and a black widow spider "sunk its fangs into his manhood." The article further elaborates that the man "spent four days in agony in hospital" and had not had what you would call an active love life since that time. Also, he had developed a deep-seated fear of portable toilets, although *The Sun,* getting both sides of the story, did quote a spokesman for the toilet suppliers: "Never

---

[8]Guys: Do not even *think* about this.

before has this happened in the history of portable toilets."

I am not criticizing the spider, here. It was simply defending its home. Suppose *you* were Mrs. Black Widow Spider, in your web, feeling safe and secure, and you had just eaten a nice meal consisting of a fly, or possibly Mr. Black Widow Spider, and you've tucked the egg sac in for a nap and are getting ready to catch forty billion winks yourself, and suddenly the roof opens up and your web, your *home,* is assaulted by a sex organ that is, relative to you, the size of the Goodyear blimp. You are going to be upset. You are going to sink your fangs first and ask questions later. But that doesn't make it any easier for the guy.

It is not just wildlife that poses a threat to guy privates. Guys are not even safe from *their own underwear.* I have here an article published in 1991 by the *South County Register* of Waldport, Oregon, headlined:

MAN WINS LAWSUIT AFTER
PRIVATES ARE "LABELED"

The article reported that this guy purchased some new underwear at a department store, wore them to bed, and awoke to discover that the underwear inspection label—this particular pair had been inspected by Number 12—was stuck to his personal organ. He could *not* get it off.

So he had to take his organ to a medical clinic. I bet

*that* was fun. I bet he *really* enjoyed explaining the situation to the receptionist, especially if the clinic was crowded that day and the receptionist was the kind of person who liked to make jokes. ("Look on the bright side, sir! At least it passed inspection!" *Loud laughter from the other patients in the reception area.*)

The clinic was able, using solvents, to remove the label. But then, the article tells us, the guy developed "a severe rash," and although the rash did respond to treatment, the guy was eventually left with "a permanent scar the size and shape of the inspection label."

There probably are some guys who might try to turn this kind of thing to their advantage, especially in singles bars ("Hi! Wanna see my label?"). But this guy, who was a lawyer,[9] sued the department store, claiming that he had been "made a laughingstock" within his family ("So, Morton, you devil, when are you going to let us *meet* this Number 12?"). He wound up collecting three thousand dollars, which makes me wonder if I would still have a legal case against the Nixon estate.

The ultimate example of an unfortunate guy medical emergency is of course the famous one involving John Bobbitt, whose wife, Lorena, cut off his penis with a knife, then drove off with it and threw it out the car window.[10] Fortunately the police were able to track

---

[9]Not that this makes it any less tragic.

[10]Thereby simultaneously exposing herself to a charge of littering, and her husband to a charge of indecent exposure.

down the penis[11] and take it to the hospital, where it was placed in a lineup with five other penises so Mr. Bobbitt could identify it.

No, really, it was surgically reattached to Mr. Bobbitt, and this incident became a huge national news event. For weeks, every time you turned on the TV, there was a perky female news anchorperson smiling cheerfully and using the phrase "cut off his penis with a kitchen knife" at every possible opportunity. ("We have a cold front moving into Virginia, the very state where John Bobbitt's wife *cut off his penis with a kitchen knife*.") U.S. industrial output dropped sharply because so many guys were walking around with both hands over their privates.

Today, of course, John Bobbitt's penis is a major celebrity with its own agent and a successful show-business career.[12] This particular penis is far better known than the U.S. vice president.[13] Nevertheless this was a chilling incident for guys, and I for one think we are *way* overdue for a federal ban on the sale or possession of kitchen knives. I also think that, just in case, we should have mandatory registration of Salad Shooters.

I am going to end this chapter on special guy medical concerns by presenting an:

---

[11]Even though it was not labeled (rim shot).
[12]Why not? It's more talented than anybody on *Melrose Place*.
[13]What's-his-name.

## Idea for Getting Really Rich

Start a Guy Medical Center. The center's motto could be: *Prostate? What prostate?*

The doctors would all be guys who had been specially trained to deal with guys' unique medical needs. Guys would not be afraid to come to this center for treatment, because they'd know they'd get the kind of medical attention they want:

DOCTOR: So, what seems to be the problem?

PATIENT: Well, the main thing is, I keep coughing up blood. Plus I have these open sores all over my body. Also I have really severe chest pains and double vision, and from time to time these little worms burrow out of my skin.

DOCTOR: It's just a sprain.

PATIENT: That's what I thought.

# 7
# Guys and Violence
## The Curse of the Noogie Gene

I HAVE HERE an article[1] that appeared in the *San Francisco Chronicle*, headlined:

### NAPA WRITER BLAMES MALENESS FOR CRIME

The article concerns an author named June Stephenson, who wrote a book entitled—this is a real title—*Men Are Not Cost Effective.* Ms. Stephenson's

---

[1]This article was written by Ron Sonenshine and sent in by alert reader Thomas William McGarry, who will receive, as a token of my gratitude, the Hope Diamond.

basic point, according to the article, is that crime is basically a male problem; that males do not become criminals because of environmental or societal influences, but simply because they are male.

"I am not saying that all men are criminals," she is quoted as saying. "But most criminals are, in fact, men."

The article says she believes that "such experiences as circumcision early in life may lead to violent behavior."

(Let me just note here parenthetically that if you want to see violent behavior in a guy, try to circumcise him *late* in life.)

But here is the key point: According to the article, Stephenson proposes "that men—not women—should bear the cost of imprisonment, perhaps through a special tax."

So it has come to this: *a tax on guys.*

I suppose it was inevitable that somebody would propose this, because guys do have a reputation for resorting to violence. But is this reputation warranted? Is it fair to say that violence is a guy problem, simply because women hardly ever do anything more violent than chop celery, whereas guys tend to sometimes lose their tempers; maybe throw a few thoughtless punches on occasion; maybe even fire a gun in anger or invade a neighboring country or go up in airplanes and drop thousands of powerful bombs on urban areas?

Okay, so guys *do* seem to have a violence problem. Maybe June Stephenson is right: Maybe there *should* be a special tax on guys to pay for the prison system. But let's be fair, here: If we're going to tax guys for prisons, shouldn't we also tax women for the extra costs that *they* impose upon society? For example, scientists estimate that, just since 1980, the American public has spent a combined total of 875,000,000,000,000,000,000,000,000 hours unsuccessfully trying to make a final decision regarding where to put furniture. It is not guys who are responsible for this. As I stated in the introduction to this book, if guys were in charge of positioning furniture, they'd leave it wherever it was. Most of the world's furniture would still be back in ancient Greece.

We should also consider the fact that certain genders consume *way* more of certain precious resources than certain other genders. To name just one area: If everybody were a guy, the human race could easily be able to get by on less than one-twentieth the current number of shoes.

And let's talk about phone-line usage. Let's consider how much of our nation's precious telephone resources are tied up at any given moment by women trying to make joint decisions on issues such as how to celebrate a close friend's fortieth birthday. A *lot* of phone resources, that's how much. Because two women making this kind of decision will want to discuss *every aspect* of the situation, including how the friend feels about getting older, and how *they* both feel about getting older, and how everybody they *know* feels about getting older, and whether the friend might want a smaller gathering, and if so who should be invited, and who should *not* be invited, and how these people will *feel* about not being invited, and how *they* would feel if they were not invited, and so maybe it should be a slightly *larger* gathering, and how their friend might *feel* about a slightly larger gathering, and how *they* might feel about a slightly larger gathering, and what kind of food they should have, and whether they should try for mainly low-fat hors d'oeuvres, or whether their friend would assume that they were having low-fat hors d'oeuvres because she was gaining weight, so maybe they should have *high*-fat hors d'oeuvres, to suggest that they hadn't *noticed* that she was gaining weight, although this might seem insensitive, so perhaps the best thing would be to have a combination of low- *and* high-fat hors d'oeuvres, or maybe even to go with exclusively *medium*-fat hors d'oeuvres, but cut them into smallish pieces, although this might make their friend think they were just being cheap, so maybe they should blah blah blah blah blah blah on into telephone eternity. Two women could waste *dozens* of potentially productive hours on this effort, and that total could easily rise into the hundreds if the issue of centerpieces comes up.

In contrast, two guys, in the identical situation,

would waste virtually *no* time on this problem, because they would handle it via the logical, efficient, and cost-effective guy technique of never having the faintest clue when *anybody's* birthday is. They wouldn't realize that their close friend had turned forty until well after he had turned forty-five.

Thus we see that there are major economic costs associated with women,[2] so it's only fair that if we're going to tax guys to pay a special tax for the prisons, then we should also tax women to pay for the costs they impose on society when they engage in wasteful behavior. For starters, we could tax June Stephenson a flat seventy-five thousand dollars for each copy of *Men Are Not Cost Effective.*

But I am drifting away from the main point of this chapter, which is Guys and Violence. Guys are violent, yes. No question about it. If you don't believe that, all you have to do is go to a football game, and you'll see guys slamming into each other, beating on each other, knocking each other to the ground with tremendous force. And that's just the guy *fans.* The guy players are *brutal.*

What makes guys so violent? To answer this question, we must consider the genetic makeup of the human guy. As you are no doubt aware, each of your body cells contain a tiny molecule (or "atom") called

[2]Notice that I have the class not to mention toilet paper.

"DNA," which stands for "DinohydroNuclearsome-thingsofAmerica." These DNA molecules in turn contain strings of small electrons called "genes" that provide, in secret code,[3] all the information required to make you an individual person, such as hair color, shoe size, and social security number.

The key is that certain genes are specific to men or women. For example, all women have a gene that makes them want to have a special bar of soap in the guest bathroom that everybody is afraid to use. Likewise, all men have a gene that scientists believe is directly related to violence.

To help you get a clearer picture of what I am talking about, consider the following scientific diagram of a guy DNA molecule:

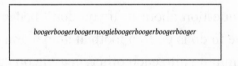

Fig. 1:  Guy DNA Molecule (shown actual size)

If you study this molecule closely using sensitive scientific instruments such as your eyeballs, you will see, cleverly encoded in it, the root cause of guy violence: the Noogie Gene. This gene—which is virtually never found in women[4]—gets its name from the fact

---

[3]To prevent others species, such as raccoons, from stealing it.
[4]With Roseanne being a big (har!) exception.

that, among other things, it causes a guy to be seized from time to time with the overpowering urge to grab another guy's head and rub his knuckles into it. Yes, this is a savage and brutal instinct, but for millions of years it has been vital to the survival of the species.[5] You see the same behavior all the time in nature, where, for example, guy wolves will constantly try to give each other noogies as the wolf pack establishes its pecking order.[6] (Certain types of guy marsupials will also snap towels.)

Unfortunately, the Noogie Gene has no place in modern, civilized society, where it can create serious problems such as violent crime and genocide and radio car-dealership commercials. Also, we now know that many commercial-airline disasters that were officially blamed on "wind shear" were in fact caused by the co-pilot—in flagrant defiance of FAA regulations[7] —giving a noogie to the pilot during takeoff. And the world will not soon forget the tragic events that ensued in 1991 when Iraq decided to give a giant interna-tional noogie to Kuwait.

What can be done about this unfortunate facet of the guy biological makeup? One obvious solution, of course, is to surgically remove all the Noogie Genes

[5]Don't ask me why.
[6]These happen to be rare Arctic pecking wolves.
[7]Which clearly state, in volume IX, article 7, section 3.2.4: "No noogies below 15,000 feet."

from every single one of the billions of cells in the guy's body, using tweezers. Phil Donahue had this operation. But it would be impractical to perform it on the guy population at large.

No, the answer is not to try to remove the Noogie Gene: The answer is to provide a safe outlet for the resultant behavior, to channel the noogie energy into some activity that is relatively harmless, such as bowling or national defense. Any activity that involves knocking things down, blowing things up, setting things on fire, or making loud noises is ideal for noogie transference.

When I lived in Pennsylvania, my auto mechanic was a guy named Ed, a bearded guy with an intense gaze and a serious temper. I believe that Ed would have been a major threat to society, except for the fact that he was *deeply* into fireworks. He bought them in huge quantities. He dissected them and studied them intently in his auto shop. He was able to make time for this activity by hardly ever working on cars. I regularly visited Ed's shop to see if he had made any progress on my Camaro. I had a 1975 Camaro that I kept at Ed's shop on basically a full-time basis for the better part of a year, in case Ed ever had a spare moment or two to fix the transmission.

On one memorable visit to Ed's, I arrived to find a sign on the door that said CLOSED. This didn't faze me;

this sign was mounted permanently on the door,[8] as part of Ed's ongoing customer-avoidance program.

I opened the door and went inside the shop. The air was thick with fireworks smoke. You couldn't see across the room.

"Ed?" I shouted, into the cloud. "It's me! Dave! I was wondering if maybe you had a chance to . . ."

Then I heard a popping sound, and I looked down, and a little cardboard tank was scuttling toward me through the blue smoke haze, emitting a shower of sparks and sporadically shooting its little cannon. And back in the gloom I could just make out the shape of Ed, watching the tank critically.

"I just got these from Ohio," he said. "I don't think they're as good as the tanks I got from Tennessee, do you? Not as loud." Ed really likes loud.

"Ed," I said, "any word on the Camaro transmission?"

"If you want to hear *loud*," Ed answered, "Listen to *this*."

And he lit what appeared to be a stick of dynamite and tossed it onto the floor, and

# *BLAM*

(This explosion is still ringing in my ears, despite the fact that it occurred in 1983.)

[8] I am not making this up.

"How about *that*," Ed said.

"That was great, Ed," I said. "Listen, do you think there's any chance that the Camaro . . ."

"I got something to show you," Ed said. "I got a . . . wait a minute."

He went over and peered out the window suspiciously. Somebody had just driven up to the shop. Ed *hated* it when strangers came around, because they were always trying to get him to fix their cars. But whoever it was saw the CLOSED sign and drove away.

Turning back to me, Ed said, "I got a hot-glue gun."

"Is that something you need to fix the Camaro?" I asked.

Ed laughed pretty hard at that. That was a good one, all right. Fix the Camaro. Har! No wonder I was a professional humorist!

It turned out that the function of the hot-glue gun was to enable Ed to *manufacture his own fireworks.* Fireworks that were *much* bigger, *much* louder than the ones he was getting from these weenies in Tennessee and Ohio. I saw Ed test-fire one of those babies once, and I can tell you that if those radical Muslim fundamentalist terrorists had had Ed on their team in 1992, the World Trade Center would now be referred to as the World Trade Pit.

But my point is that fireworks were good for Ed, and society in general, because they gave him a relatively harmless outlet for his Noogie-Gene tendencies, which were exacerbated by the tension that constantly built inside him from the strain and hassle of being in the demanding business of not fixing cars.

I believe that without such a release, guys can become dangerous. You know what the neighbors always say about the guy who suddenly goes berserk and massacres everybody in a Burger King with a machine gun just because he's sick and tired of trying to open those stupid little packets of ketchup with his teeth.[9] The neighbors always say: "He was such a quiet person!" And they might very well add: "He never set off fireworks!"

So when we see guys engaging in what appear to be stupid, pointless, wasteful, destructive, and juvenile activities such as deliberately driving a car into a lake, or carrying a piano all the way to the top of a six-story building so they can find out what happens when they push it off the roof, or shooting marine flares into pumpkins, we should not condemn them. We should *congratulate* them for finding legal and socially acceptable and usually nonfatal ways to release their violent impulses.

This is why I believe that the Nobel-Peace-Prize-Handing-Out Committee should consider giving a large cash award to the guys who belong to the Chicagoland Corvair Enthusiasts club, for their pioneering efforts in

[9]Not that I entirely disagree with him.

the area of making vacuum cleaners explode. I am not making up these efforts; I have personally viewed them on a wonderful videotape that was sent to me by Larry Claypool and Kirk Parro, who are members of the Chicagoland Corvair Enthusiasts.

(Perhaps you are thinking that people who are enthusiastic, in an organized way, about Corvairs are perhaps—to use a psychological term—several drawers shy of a file cabinet. Let me assure you that you are correct.)

Here's the background: One day Claypool and Parro were reading a publication called *CORSA Communiqué*, which is the official magazine of the Corvair Society of America, and they came across an article headlined:

VACUUM CLEANERS AND SIPHONS DON'T MIX

The article was written by a person named Chess Earman,[10] who recounted what happened once when he was trying to siphon the gasoline out of one of his four Corvairs.[11] He didn't want to get gasoline in his mouth, so he decided to get the suction going by holding the end of the siphon hose up against a vacuum-cleaner hose. What this meant, of course, is that he was sucking gas fumes directly into an electric motor, which as you know operates by having sparks fly

---

[10] This is a real name.
[11] Yes: *four.*

around inside it. So the next thing Chess Earman knew, there was an explosion inside the vacuum cleaner, and fire was coming out of the back of it "like a jet engine."

Fortunately Earman was able to unplug the vacuum cleaner before anything really bad happened. But this was indeed a chilling cautionary story about the extreme danger of messing around with gasoline and vacuum cleaners, and when Larry Claypool and Kirk Parro read it, their natural reaction, as guys, was: Hey, *cool.*

"Such a challenge must not go unmet," is how they put it, in a letter to me.

And thus it came to pass that, for a number of years during the 1980s, the big attraction at the annual Fourth of July picnic of the Chicagoland Corvair Enthusiasts was the Flaming Vacuum Cleaner competition. I wish you could see the videotape, because it is difficult for me, using mere words, to convey the full flavor of this event. But I will try.

Each year, contestants brought vacuum cleaners, which were grouped into teams under signs denoting their brands (TEAM HOOVER, TEAM ELECTROLUX, etc.). One by one, these vacuum cleaners were brought out into the competition arena, where they were introduced by the announcer over the public-address system.[12] The

---

[12]Of *course* they had a public-address system.

vacuum-cleaner nozzle would be placed in a shallow pan of gasoline. Then everybody would retreat to a safe distance, and the vacuum cleaner would be plugged in to a 240-volt power source, causing the motor to start, so that gasoline was being sucked in through the nozzle.

Usually nothing happened for a few seconds; then there'd usually be a BANG and the vacuum cleaner would jump a few inches into the air. This always got a cheer from the crowd. Various things would happen next, depending on the vacuum cleaner. Some models would emit a cloud of black smoke and stop running, causing the crowd to boo. But other models would send a jet of flame shooting several feet out the back for several seconds. A few hardy models kept running for several minutes; the longer they'd run, the more the crowd would cheer, encouraged by the announcer. Sometimes the flames would stop, and inevitably you'd hear somebody—it always sounds like the same guy, a guy who has been drinking a *lot* of beer—shout "MORE GAS!" Certain canister models—these were the most popular with the crowd, getting wild cheers of approval—would explode violently apart, with the tops flying up and out of the camera's range of view.

"The canister tops often exceeded altitudes of thirty feet," report Claypool and Parro.

After each contestant was finished, it would be dragged off and dumped onto a growing, smoking mound of charred and mangled machinery, and the announcer would say something nice about it, such as, "Not bad, Electrolux Number Two!" Or: "Let's hear it for the Eureka!"

On the tape, between contestants, you occasionally see women walk past in front of the camera, on their way to get more potato salad or something; they sometimes look at the guys, who are working industriously away the way guys do when they're on a Mission, getting another vacuum cleaner ready for action, and the women shake their heads in such a way as to clearly indicate that, yes, they knew guys could be idiots, but they had never before realized that guys could be idiots of this *magnitude*.

Again, these women did not understand that the Flaming Vacuum Cleaner competition was, in fact, a relatively *positive* activity for guys to engage in—that if the guys didn't have this outlet, they could easily become involved in something with far more serious consequences. I am sure that none of us ever wants to pick up our morning newspaper and read a headline that says CHICAGO FEARED VAPORIZED IN MISHAP INVOLVING EXPERIMENTAL NUCLEAR-POWERED CORVAIR.

No, the Flaming Vacuum Cleaner competition was probably a good thing. I want to stress, however, that it was also a very dangerous thing, not to be attempted by amateurs. Remember that the guys who did it were not ordinary untrained civilians: They were *Corvair en-*

*thusiasts.* And they took certain critical safety precautions, such as rigging up a public-address system. You must remember that gasoline and vacuum cleaners do *not* mix, and under no circumstances should you attempt to do anything like this yourself. And if you do, please let me know where and when.

# 8

# The Domestic Side of Guys (With a Side Discussion on Orgasms)

*or:* The Secret Truth About Why
Guys Are Better at Math
*or:* Where Standards Came From
*or:* Perfectly Legitimate Reasons
Why a Person Might Elect to Blow His
Nose on His Laundry
*or:* Let's Not Be So Darned Critical
of Tapeworms

PROBABLY the fastest-growing sector of the U.S. economy is the sector that conducts surveys asking women what is wrong with men. About every two days you read yet another newspaper article stating that 92.7 percent of American women find men to be pathetically inadequate in some way, with the two major areas of male deficiency being:

- Housework
- Orgasms

When I say "orgasms," I of course am not suggesting that *guys* don't have orgasms. Guys have *plenty* of orgasms. Most guys have more orgasms in *a single day* (and here I am thinking of a day that probably occurred during the summer between ninth and tenth grades) than some women (and here I am thinking of Margaret Thatcher) have in their entire *lifetimes.*

No, the big complaint that women have is that guys often fail to *induce* orgasms. This is because the guy biological makeup, as I explained in chapter 2, is designed to ensure the survival of the human race by giving guys the ability to achieve orgasms virtually instantaneously with virtually any kind of stimulus (although here I am not thinking of Margaret Thatcher).

This ability was vitally important millions of years ago, when primitive humans lived in a hostile environment. Back then, a guy could not afford to engage in a lot of time-wasting sentimental foreplay such as kissing, hugging, stroking, putting down the haunch of meat he was gnawing on, etc. A guy had to immediately achieve orgasm with the female (or, if a female was not available, with his hand, or a prehistoric *Playboy* magazine[1]) so that he'd be ready to fight off predators or hunt game or take a biologically important nap.

Unfortunately, in modern times the ability to have quick orgasms and then fall asleep is no longer as

[1]This month's featured spread: "The Girls of the Paleolithic Era."

prized as it once was, especially among women. When modern women describe the qualities they're looking for in the ideal man, the phrase "a real fast ejaculator" is usually pretty far down the list, right after "a large amount of nasal hair."

Thus we have a fundamental disparity between the sexual needs of men and women, as is shown in the following table:

Average Time Required to Achieve Orgasm

| Men | Fruit Flies | Women |
|---|---|---|
| 2.3 | 4.7 | 5.6 |
| *(measured in seconds)* | *(measured in seconds)* | *(measured in episodes of "General Hospital")* |

This disparity causes a lot of unhappiness, because when a man and a woman are trying to have sex, he will often climax before she is ready. Sometimes he will climax before she is, technically, in the room.

Naturally, guys get *all* the blame for this problem. You'd think that, just once, a leading public figure (and here I am thinking of the secretary of commerce) would get up at a press conference and say, "Hey! Women! Let's try to have faster orgasms so that everybody will have more time to grow the economy and create needed jobs, not to mention watch Monday Night Football!"

But no. As is so often the case, the responsibility for

changing is placed entirely on the shoulders of guys. So over the years, guys have developed a variety of techniques for delaying orgasm, with one major category being

## PHYSICAL TECHNIQUES

The most effective physical technique, one that has been honed to perfection over the years by some of the world's greatest lovers (and here I am thinking of my friend Tom Shroder, who told me about it) is when the guy, just as he is about to climax, bangs his head violently into an iron bed railing and raises a head knot the size of a golf ball. Another effective physical technique is when, at the critical moment, the guy's dog, which has padded silently into the bedroom and which has a nose-surface temperature of forty-six degrees below zero, decides that this would be a good time to sniff the guy's bare butt:

GUY: . . . yes, yes, yes . . .

WOMAN: . . . yes, yes, yesyesyes . . .

GUY: . . . yesyesyesyesyes *YEOOOOWWWWWW*

Of course physical techniques are not practical in every situation, such as when a guy is really hitting it off with his date, but they have decided to go to *her* place. ("Do you mind if we stop at my apartment first? I need to pick up my dog.") This is why guys wishing to delay reaching orgasm have also had to develop certain

## MENTAL TECHNIQUES

The primary one is the **Mathematics Technique,** which is when the guy tries to distract himself during sex by solving a math problem. This technique is the reason why, over the years, most of your breakthrough mathematical discoveries have been made by guys. It has nothing to do with guys being naturally better at math; it has to do with guys frantically trying to *think* about math to take their minds off the fact that they are having sex. (You don't actually *believe* that Isaac Newton was sitting under an apple tree when he figured out gravity, do you? Give me a *break.*)

The problem with the Mathematics Technique is that, what with the overall decline in U.S. academic skills, a lot of guys can't solve math problems without calculators, which, even if used in a suave and subtle manner, can suck the romance right out of a moment. This is why more guys are using the alternative technique of **Picturing Something Really Nonappealing, and Here I Am Once Again Thinking of Margaret Thatcher, or in Extreme Cases, Rush Limbaugh in a Thong-Style Bathing Suit.**

My point here is that a lot of guys are making a tremendous and sometimes painful effort to be more effective at satisfying their mates, and yet they are still, according to generally accepted standards of sexual performance, considered to be pitifully inadequate. And do you know why? Because *women set the standards,* that's why. And I'm not just talking about sexual standards; I'm talking about *all* standards.

This is because women *invented* standards. It happened on a fateful day millions of years ago, when all the primitive guys were out in the forest doing some important guy thing such as hunting wild game or picking their noses with spears. Back in the village, the women were pounding roots to make them tender enough to be thrown away, when suddenly one of them, who was known as Smart Woman, said to the others: "You know what we need around here? We need some *standards.*"

And the other women said, "Yes. What are 'standards'?"

And Smart Woman said, "Standards are when we say to our mates, 'Don't do something.' For example, we could say, 'No peeing in the cave.' "

And the other women, amazed, said, "We could *say* that?"

And Smart Woman said, "Why not?"

"But why would our mates obey us?" asked the other women.

"Because," said Smart Woman, "we will look at them in a Certain Way." And she demonstrated a new facial expression that she had been working on; an expression that only women can make; an expression that has the mysterious power to make men realize that they are in Big Trouble, without knowing exactly why.

"Wow," said the other women, deeply impressed. Then one of them said, "How about, 'No gnawing on a fish during sex'? Can that be a standard?"

"Certainly," said Smart Woman.

And another woman said, "Can we say, 'No playing the hilarious[2] joke where you creep up to your mate and put your face directly in front of hers and open your mouth wide to reveal that you have a mastodon eyeball in there'?"

"Of course," said Smart Woman.

And another woman said, "And a standard that says, 'No migrating all the way across the land bridge to what will eventually be known as North America without stopping once to go to the bathroom'?"

"Yes!" said Smart Woman. "We can make *any standards we want.* We can even establish standards for personal hygiene!"

"What is 'personal hygiene?' " asked the other women.

"Personal hygiene," said Smart Woman, "is, for example, 'No storing meat in your armpit.' "

"Wow," said the other women.

[2]This marked the invention of sarcasm.

So when the guys got back to the village, they received a severe shock.

"What do you *mean*, no peeing in the cave?" they said. "We *always* pee in the cave!"

But the women gave them a Certain Look, and instantly the guys realized that, unless they followed the new standards, their delicate primitive social fabric was going to be strained, plus they were not going to get any nooky for the next 2.3 million years. So although they did not *understand* the standards, they did their bumbling best to follow them.

This is basically where we stand today. The only difference is, we have *way* more standards. As we have noted, there are standards for sexual performance that are ludicrously incompatible with the guy biological makeup. There are social standards involving being sensitive, remembering anniversaries, listening during conversations, not farting loud on purpose, and not going away for six or eight months at a time without at least leaving a note. There are *thousands* of standards for domestic life, involving such totally alien (to guys) concepts as curtains, bedspreads, napkins, butter dishes, hors d'oeuvres, ceramic cat figurines, salad forks, hand towels, chafing dishes, floral arrangements, tablecloths, shelving paper, coasters, linen closets, throw rugs, room deodorizers, hangers, irons, little soaps shaped like fruit, and decorative boxes to hold tissues that already come in a perfectly good box. To name just a few.

Guys, left on their own in the wild, will develop life-styles that do not involve *any* of these things. I base this statement on my own personal experience living as a bachelor in an apartment in West Chester, Pennsyl-vania, with my friend Randall Shantz. When we moved in, we looked around at our apartment, which was barren and sterile, devoid of furniture, and we realized what we needed: a hockey game. So we got one, the kind with little men who spin and flail around while you frantically work the levers and curse at the men for being so inept. This was the centerpiece of our living room.

Of course we soon had other furnishings. These con-sisted of some folding lawn chairs, a TV set, and a rab-bit named Flyer, who could drink beer and poop an estimated 584,000,000,000,000,000 small, hard pel-lets per day. That was pretty much it, decor-wise. It never would have occurred to us to go out and pay money for something to put over the windows, or a special dish to put butter on. For one thing, we didn't have butter. We never had anything in our refrigerator except beer and cartons of Wawa brand iced tea, which we generally had for breakfast along with some nutri-tional Marlboro brand cigarettes. I believe we had one plate, a white one, which we kept in the sink, ready to be rinsed off for those formal occasions that required a plate, such as when we couldn't find an ashtray. We had our dinners catered by the New Haven Style Pizza[3] takeout department; we ate from boxes while watching TV.

Other than rinsing the plate and sweeping up the rabbit doots when company was coming, we did very little housecleaning, because we had very few things to clean. We left the bathrooms pretty much alone, our theory being that when the fungal growths reached a certain size and aggressiveness level, we would find a new apartment.

It was a simple lifestyle, one that provided us with all the basic comforts, yet at the same time was uncluttered enough that we could play Indoor Ricochet Death Frisbee. Of course by even the most basic standards of domesticity, Randall and I were living like savages. But we honestly didn't know this, because we were guys, and guys in their natural state simply are not *aware* of domestic standards, in the same sense that fish are not aware of the stock market.

This is the profoundly ignorant state that the typical guy is in when he enters into a domestic arrangement with a woman. He has maybe four domestic standards ("No spitting in bed," for example), and she has hundreds, perhaps thousands of them. She has strict standards concerning which pillowcases go with which

[3]"You've Tried the Rest; Now Try the Best."

sheets; he has slept on a naked pillow for years, ever since the time he used his lone pillowcase to wipe off his motorcycle after he washed it in the shower.

(I have been married, off and on, since 1969, and I *still* do not grasp the point of making the bed.)

The woman and the guy have profoundly different concepts of "clean." When the woman "cleans" a bathroom, she will go in there with numerous specialized products and implements for cleansing, scouring, shining, and deodorizing the glass, porcelain, and tile. She will spend hours just on the "grout." She will eradicate dirt on the molecular level. She will track down and destroy each individual mildew spore. She can actually *hear* germs, and she can make them scream. She will leave the commode clean enough to be used in a surgical procedure. Whereas the guy, if instructed to clean the bathroom, will go in there with a single paper towel and the first spray bottle he finds. It might be Windex, or it might be Raid. The guy will spend about three minutes in the bathroom, squirting stuff randomly out of his spray bottle and then wiping it up with his towel. He will pay no attention to whether or not he is actually getting the bathroom cleaner. There could be a dead human body lying in the bathtub, and the guy would spray and wipe it.

Perhaps you think I am exaggerating the domesticity gap between guys and women. If so, perhaps you will be interested in the following actual letter I received:

Dear Dave,

I need your opinion. My girlfriend is trying to change me. She doesn't like the way I live, while I see it as practical and efficient.

First of all, she doesn't like the way I blow my nose on my dirty clothes. Whenever I have a cold, rather than waste $1.50 on a box of Kleenex, I blow my nose on a pair of dirty pants or a shirt in my laundry hamper. The way I see it, the clothes are already dirty, and they're going to get washed soon anyway. What's the big deal? My girlfriend says it's "gross."

Also, I was recently cooking a batch of Sloppy Joes, and while I was draining the grease, some of it dripped on the kitchen floor. Rather than fooling around with the hot grease, I told her I'd let it congeal overnight and scrape it off in the morning with the paint scraper. Of course she went crazy. You would have thought I suggested going out and inhaling asbestos fibers.

Lastly, I tend to let my newspapers pile up. I put them in grocery bags and they sit in my apartment. My girlfriend keeps nagging me to take them to the recycling center, but I've discovered that I can arrange the bags to create furniture. Not only have I saved myself some gas money, but I've new brown hard furniture to boot. I don't actually use the couch much, but I've found I can set a hell of a lot of beer bottles on it. So please, help my relationship. Am I out of line, or am I simply logical and practical?

Sincerely,

Brian Robinson
Portland, Oregon

Being as objective as is humanly possible without a sex-change operation, I have to side with Brian on this one. I mean, compared with a lot of guys, he is Martha Stewart in the domesticity department. He has garbage bags. He can cook Sloppy Joes. *He has a laundry hamper.* And yet because of a few minor deviations from The Standards, his entire lifestyle is under attack.

And while we're on the topic of women being pretty harsh with guys, let us consider the following excerpt from a letter sent by Alison Schuler of Albuquerque,[4] New Mexico:

> My husband announced one morning that he had discovered the previous night, on the eve of a two-day business trip, that he was out of underwear. Why he told me, I do not know. I never tell *him* when *I'm* out of underwear. Anyway, he decided to remedy the situation in true guy fashion, by washing exactly three sets of underwear, thus disregarding the bulging hamper full of the rest of his underwear, which, presumably, would wash itself during his absence.

This is a perfect example of the kind of hurtful stereotypical blanket statement[5] about guys that women, as a group, are always making. Just because Ms. Schuler's husband doesn't do the entire laundry, doesn't mean that there aren't millions upon millions

[4]Motto: "The City That Is Probably Spelled Wrong."
[5]Another one is: "Guys always hog the blanket."

of males who *do* do the laundry, then hang it out to dry under the three suns of the Planet Xoomar, where they live. I will admit, however, that most guys here on Earth do not do any more laundry than they absolutely have to. A single-sock load would not be out of the question, for a guy. A guy might well choose to wash *only the really dirty part* of the sock.

Why is this? Are guys simply worthless, irresponsible scum? Yes, but that is not the cause of laundry impairment. The cause of their impairment is that guys, even when they have learned that they *should* do laundry, are *afraid* to do it, especially laundry belonging to people of other genders, because they know they will probably get into, once more, Big Trouble. The problem is that women usually own a lot of sensitive garments with laundering-instruction tags full of strict instructions like:

DO NOT MACHINE-WASH. DO NOT USE BLEACH. DO NOT USE HOT WATER. DO NOT USE WARM WATER. DO NOT USE ANY WATER. DO NOT EVEN TOUCH THIS GARMENT UNLESS YOU ARE WEARING STERILIZED SURGICAL GLOVES. PUT THIS GARMENT DOWN IMMEDIATELY, YOU CLUMSY OAF.

I'm deeply intimidated by such instructions. I developed my laundering skills in college, where I used what laundry scientists call the Pile System, wherein you put your dirty undershorts on the floor until they form a waist-high pile, thus subjecting the bottom shorts to intense heat and pressure that causes them to become, over several months, clean enough to wear if you're desperate and spray them with Right Guard brand deodorant. When I lived with Randall, we fed our laundry to large carnivorous coin-operated machines in the basement, and threw away whatever clothes didn't fit when we were done. This is why most married guys use the Hamper System, which is similar to the Pile System except that the clothes really do get clean, thanks to magical hamper rays.

I am jesting, of course. I realize that hamperized clothes are in fact cleaned by a person such as Alison Schuler of Albuquerque, New Mexico. But I also know that women follow a complex procedure involving sorting and presoaking and twenty-seven different combinations of water temperatures and chemical compounds such as fabric softener, stain remover, fabric hardener, cream rinse, ointments, suppositories, enriched plutonium, etc. A woman wouldn't let a guy do her laundry unless he underwent *years* of training, because she assumes he'd screw it up and cause her garments to shrink down to cute little Tinkerbell clothes, or transmaterialize in the dryer, similar to what happened to that unfortunate man in the movie *The Fly*, so she'd wind up with, for example, a brassiere that had pants legs.

This is why women are reluctant to let men near the

laundry, as was shown by a nationwide survey of several women I know. A typical reaction came from my research department, Judi Smith, who gave the following statement regarding her husband, Tim, a Ph.D. college professor: "I don't trust him to do my laundry at *all*, unless I've sorted it first and given him strict instructions before each and every load, because otherwise everything we own would be mauve or gray. . . . He puts his clothes away damp. He can't put away anyone else's clothes, because he can't fold. I mean, the man can't fold a *towel* for God's sake. Somehow, he can't get the corners to match up. A *hand* towel, even."

I'm not defending guys here. I'm just saying that a lot of us have developed a powerful laundry phobia, and we will continue to suffer from it as long as women roll their eyes and shove us away from the washing machine when we're about to, for example, wash our delicate silks in the same load as our boat cover. This is also true of the other major domestic areas such as cleaning and cooking and remembering where, exactly, we left the children. Yes, we guys have problems in these areas, but this is *not our fault.* We are talking about *nature* here. It's a lot like tapeworms. Tapeworms tend to not have a positive public image, because they are repulsive organisms that get inside people's intestines and eat people's food and grow to lengths of sixty feet and have millions of repulsive little babies. But is this their "fault"? *No!* It is their *nature!*

And guys are no different! Guys are *exactly like* tape-worms, except for being slightly less likely to help with the dishes.

That is why I am asking you women to please try to be more understanding. When you look at the guy in your life, lying on the sofa and burping sporadically in the direction of a football game even though you have asked him fourteen times to please take out the garbage, do not think critical and contemptuous thoughts. Instead, think of two words that will remind you of the deep-rooted problems that he is struggling, deep inside, to overcome; two words that will help you, in some small way, to feel his pain. Those words are of course "intestinal parasite."

Women, with your help and understanding, we guys can do better. And we *will* do better. We will, inch by painful inch, overcome our natural handicaps, and we will rise to meet your standards for personal behavior. It will not happen tomorrow, or the next day, or the day after that, or even necessarily before the Earth crashes back into the sun. But it *will* happen, because we guys are sick and tired of not living up to your expectations, and we are by gosh really going to start trying to change.

But not until after the play-offs.

# 9
## Guys in Action

OVER THE YEARS, guys have taken a lot of vicious abuse.[1] Guys have been blamed for just about every terrible thing that has ever happened, including war, genocide, and bass-fishing tournaments.

Granted, we deserve it. But there is another side to the guy coin. It happens that there are also countless guys who have really Made a Difference; guys who have performed feats of unsung heroism; guys who—

[1]Especially in this book.

when Old Man Trouble reared his head and somebody needed to *take action;* when it was the bottom of the ninth with two out and men on first and second and the home team trailing by two, and somebody had to step up to the plate and stroke the long ball; when it was fourth and eight with two minutes to go and there was no tomorrow for either team and it was a question of who really had the Desire and the Will to Win; when push had come to shove and it was time to separate the sheep from the goats by either cutting bait or getting off the pot; when there were no atheists in the foxhole and a penny saved was a penny earned and you had to walk eight miles to school barefoot in the snow and a loaf of bread cost a nickel, but nobody *had* a nickel and the most you could expect in your Christmas stocking was some used chewing gum, but you didn't complain, no sir, because there was a Depression going on and times were tough for everybody, not like today, when kids have Nintendo games and trust funds and they walk around in their $157 sneakers with their baseball caps on backward, which makes about as much sense as (they probably do this, too, and I *don't want to know about it*) wearing a jockstrap backward, and don't get me started on all this body-piercing going on among young people today, some of them putting rings in their *noses,* for God's sake, which does not seem sanitary at *all,* which is why, although I ordinarily do not favor government intervention into the lives of individual citizens, I feel there ought to be a federal law stating that before you get your nose pierced, you should have to take an IQ test, which would consist of one question ("Do you want to get your nose pierced?"), and if you gave the wrong answer ("Yes"), you would be legally prohibited from getting your nose pierced, and before I get a letter from some liberal Communist bleeding-heart vegetarian American Civil Liberties Union lawyer claiming that such a law would violate people's constitutional rights, let me point out that the U.S. Constitution, in Article Six, Section Four, Verse Two, specifically states "By the way, nothing in this Constitution shall be construed to mean that people have the right to wear jewelry in their noses," and to ignore the clear intent of these words by our Founding Fathers would be an insult to this nation and to its many law-abiding citizens, especially the countless unsung guys who, when Old Man Trouble reared his head—

> *WARNING WARNING WARNING*
> WE ARE NOW APPROACHING
> THE END OF THIS SENTENCE

*took action.*

I want to talk about some of those unsung guys. I want to start with the absolutely true story of a guy I happen to know personally, and how he came through in the clutch during what could have been a serious natural disaster. I'm going to call this guy "Wally" and his wife "Lynne." I am giving them aliases because this story involves the use of marijuana.[2]

Let me stress for the benefit of any impressionable young readers out there that marijuana is very, very bad. Medical research has shown that people who use marijuana are more than *eight times* as likely as non-users to eat raw cookie dough. And the figures are even more frightening for pepperoni.

But there was a time, not so long ago, when many people were unaware of these dangerous side effects, and it was during this time that Wally and Lynne used some marijuana in their home in Miami. Then they decided to spend the evening lying in bed, watching the Mel Brooks movie *The Producers* on TV.

This happened to be powerful marijuana, and Wally and Lynne were *extremely* wasted. I am certain that you, like myself and Bill Clinton, have never been in this condition, but we know from reading medical journals that a person under the influence of powerful marijuana is comparable—in terms of alertness, reaction time, problem-solving skills, and overall central-nervous-system functionality—to linoleum. A person in this condition is not capable of quick thinking and ef-

[2]Or, as it is sometimes called in modern slang lingo, "Mary Joan."

fective decision-making. People in this condition can take upwards of two hours to open a can of soda ("Do you realize that this pop tab—Just this pop tab!—is actually *billions and billions of MOLECULES??*" "My God, you're *RIGHT!*")

That is the condition that Wally and Lynne were in, watching *The Producers,* when suddenly the show was interrupted in midscene by an alarmed-looking announcer with an Urgent News Bulletin: *A major hurricane was heading directly toward Miami.*

A moment or two passed while this information worked its way into what was passing for Lynne's and Wally's consciousness.

Then:

"Oh my God," said Lynne.

"Oh my God," agreed Wally.

"Wally," said Lynne,[3] "what are we gonna *do?*"

So there it was. Wally was in the ultimate guy pressure situation: There was trouble on the way, *big* trouble, and his woman was looking to *him* to make a decision. Wally knew, even in his severely impaired state, that he had to act. The hurricane shutters needed to be closed. The yard needed to be cleared of loose objects that could, propelled by hurricane winds, become deadly missiles. Emergency supplies needed to be gathered. It might even be necessary to evacuate, as

---

[3]Who somehow had the presence of mind to use his alias.

Wally and Lynne lived in a low-lying area, near the water.

And there wasn't much time: The TV was now showing satellite photographs of the monster hurricane, moving closer, closer. Wally looked at the screen, then at Lynne, who was watching him anxiously, waiting for him to say something, *depending on him to come through.* Fighting to clear the dense fog from his brain, Wally considered the situation, and, finally, he made a decision.

"Lynne," he said, "we're gonna die."

It seemed like a solid decision. There was no way, in their condition, that they could evacuate. There was reason to doubt that they could, without assistance, remember how to open the bedroom door.

On the screen, the TV news people were sounding more and more urgent. In the bedroom, Wally and Lynne were becoming more and more distraught. They wanted, desperately, to act, but they were hopelessly nonfunctional; all they could do was wander back and forth in front of the TV, Lynne in tears, Wally tugging helplessly at his hair, both of them watching the increasingly grim newspersons deliver the increasingly bad news.

"We're gonna die," Wally repeated, so as to keep them focused on the issue at hand.

Nobody—especially not Wally and Lynne—knows how long they spent in this agony. But then, suddenly—and this is why I am darned proud to be a guy—Wally had the glimmer of an idea. Call it an inner reserve of guy strength; call it instinct; call it the Will to Live. Whatever it was, something deep inside told Wally that things could not end this way. Somehow he knew there was an answer, and if he could just concentrate hard enough, he would be able to dredge it up from the deep recesses of his brain . . . If he could just remember what it was . . . *Wait a minute* . . . YES! That's *IT*!

He turned and faced Lynne. She looked at him, tears streaming down her face. But something in his look told her that maybe—just maybe—they had a chance.

"Lynne," he said, *"we're watching a tape."*

He was right. They had forgotten that they were watching a borrowed videotape of *The Producers*. Unbeknownst to them, it had been recorded as Hurricane David approached South Florida; since this event had occurred several years earlier, the danger now posed by Hurricane David to Wally and Lynne was, mathematically, quite small.

"My God, you're *right*," said Lynne, and in her eyes there was love, and—yes—worship.

And why not? *They were going to live.*

Her guy had come through.

And that is only one true story of a guy saving the day by quick thinking. Another example, which I found out about via news articles sent in by a number of alert readers, involves an incident that occurred in Turkey on September 8, 1992. The guy in this case was a U.S. Air Force pilot who was flying an F-16C fighter jet to the northwestern corner of Iraq to patrol the "no-fly" zone there. It was supposed to be a routine mission. But when you are flying a high-performance fighter aircraft toward potentially hostile territory, nothing is ever, really, "routine."

At first there were no signs of trouble. But gradually the pilot began to sense that something was wrong. When you have flown enough missions, you develop a "gut feeling" for this type of thing, and pretty soon he knew, deep down inside, that he *really* had to pee.

This presented a problem. Your modern jet fighter plane does not contain bathrooms; these were discontinued several years ago as part of the military downsizing, which also eliminated beverage-cart service. And of course the pilot, traveling at hundreds of miles per hour, could not simply pee out the window; some pee could have landed on the Kurds, who were the very people his mission was intended to protect.

Fortunately, he had what the Air Force calls a "piddle-pack," which is a device consisting of a sponge inside a plastic container, designed to enable pilots to relieve themselves in flight. The problem was, when he unfastened his safety belt and adjusted his seat upward, the belt buckle became wedged between the seat and the control stick, causing the plane to make a sharp right turn. It began to dive, plunging from thirty-three thousand feet in a wild and deadly spin. The pilot fought to regain control, but it was hopeless; when he reached two thousand feet, with virtually no time left, he made the decision to eject, getting out just in time.

Thanks to this quick thinking, he was able to avert what could have been a real disaster. The only downside is that an eighteen-million-dollar airplane was instantly converted into landfill. But the important thing is: *He did not pee in his pants.* At least the article doesn't *say* he did. It also doesn't say what happened to the piddle-pack. I hope our side retrieved it. You wouldn't want a device of such great military value falling into enemy hands.

For our next example of Guys in Action, we go to Grant's Pass, Oregon; where some guys had what newspaper accounts described as a "rafting and outdoor group" called Mountain Men Anonymous. In May of 1993, this group was holding an initiation ritual for a potential member. Perhaps you would like to guess what the ritual consisted of. If you guessed that it was a sensitive and meaningful ceremony, wherein the guys hugged each other and played drums and shared their deepest masculine feelings, you have not been paying close attention to this book.

No, the ritual consisted of having a few beers, putting a beer can on the potential member's head, then *shooting it off with an arrow.* This is a real guy ritual. None of that wussy New Age crap for Mountain Men Anonymous. No, they have a ritual that *means* something, a ritual that will really stick in the potential member's mind, which is also what happened to the arrow in this case. It entered the potential member's head through his right eye, passed through his brain,[4] and lodged in the back of his skull.

This did not kill him. You cannot kill a *real* guy merely by shooting an arrow through his brain. He did lose the one eye, but after the doctors got the arrow out, they were amazed to discover that he had suffered no brain damage. He even held a press conference at the hospital.

"I feel really stupid," he told the press.

I think he was way too hard on himself. What he did took great courage. Too many of us, in this day and age, are content to sit back and let "the other guy" put a beer can on his head and let his friends try to shoot it off with an arrow after they have been drinking. I applaud this guy, and I applaud Mountain Men Anonymous for thinking up this ritual. If we required people to go through this type of initiation before they were allowed to participate in, for example, the New Hamp-

---

[4]Doctors confirmed that he did, in fact, have one.

shire primary, this would be a much better nation in which to live.

Speaking of guys and doctors, our next example of Guys in Action concerns two guy doctors—a surgeon and an anesthesiologist—who responded courageously to a medical situation that, without their bold and decisive action, could easily have turned out to be routine.

This occurred at the Medical Center of Central Massachusetts. According to *The Boston Globe*, an elderly woman was on the operating table, sedated, in need of emergency gall-bladder surgery. The surgeon was all ready to go. In fact, he had *been* all ready to go for an hour and a half when the anesthesiologist arrived, so he was none too happy when the anesthesiologist began boldly and decisively making coffee.

At this point, the surgeon had several options. He could:

1. Proceed with the operation as soon as possible, then hash out his disagreement with the anesthesiologist later.
2. Proceed with the operation as soon as possible, then bring the matter to the attention of the hospital authorities.
3. Proceed with the operation as soon as possible, and try to put the incident out of his mind.

The surgeon, after weighing these options, elected to:

4. Throw a medical sponge at the anesthesiologist.

This is SGP, Standard Guy Procedure, for handling anger. We know that if we bottle our petty hostilities up inside, there is a very real danger that we will, over time, forget them. So we prefer to get our anger right out into the open, where it can do some damage.

When the anesthesiologist got hit by the sponge, he realized immediately that it would be idiotic to escalate this petty incident by responding to such a childish act, so he ignored it.

Ha ha! That was of course a joke.

The anesthesiologist, as a guy, had no choice but to retaliate. There is an old saying among guys that goes: "A guy who gets hit by a sponge and does not strike back is the kind of weenie who probably also would refuse to jeopardize his life and the lives of innocent people in a confrontation over a parking space."

And so the anesthesiologist and the surgeon, in the words of *The Boston Globe*, "began punching each other and fell to the floor." Right there in the operating room. With the patient (Remember the patient?) still on the operating table.

Of course it could have been worse. The two doctors could—anything is possible, with guys defending their manhoods—have gotten into a fight *while the operation was actually going on.* This would have been really serious, because a guy in the heat of battle will strike out with whatever is at hand, and you could get a newspaper story with a headline like:

### SURGEON HELD IN ORGAN ASSAULT
#### BLUDGEONS ANESTHESIOLOGIST
#### WITH ELDERLY WOMAN'S GALL BLADDER

Fortunately, this did not happen. All that happened was that both guys were admonished and fined by the state medical board, as well as being placed on five years probation by the hospital. In other words, these guys permanently marred their professional reputations and seriously jeopardized medical careers that they had undoubtedly spent years building. But so what? The important thing is: *They did not back down.*

Our next example of Guys in Action also involves decisive response in an acute medical situation. This occurred in 1992 at the Willowbrook Golf Course in Winter Haven, Florida. According to the Associated Press account, some guys were playing a round of golf, when suddenly one of them—in the kind of shocking occurrence that we can never really be prepared for—was struck by a falling piddle pack.

No, seriously, he suffered a heart attack and, unfortunately, died, right on the sixteenth green. As you can imagine, this created a serious problem for the golfers—described by the Associated Press as the deceased's "friends and neighbors"—who were playing on the course behind him. Here, in the midst of what was to be an afternoon of sport and camaraderie, they had suddenly and tragically lost one of their own. What should they do? What is the appropriate mode of behavior when a guy is confronted with such a profoundly sad and upsetting situation?

The answer is—and I hope this will silence those who claim that guys are insensitive—the golfers *skipped the sixteenth hole.* That's right: For two hours, as the deceased's body lay on the green and police tried to locate his widow, the golfers went directly from the fifteenth hole to the seventeenth hole, making the extreme sacrifice of missing out on *a full one-eighteenth of a golf game,* so as to avoid getting into a situation wherein they would be forced to do something that could be perceived as disrespectful to their friend and neighbor, such as hitting a ball off of his body.[5]

To be sure that this was typical guy-golfer behavior, I discussed this incident with a friend of mine named Bill Rose, who is an editor at *The Miami Herald* and an avid golfer, not in that order.

I explained the setup to Bill and asked him to assume

[5]In this case, experts recommend a five iron.

he was playing golf in a foursome several holes behind the deceased.

"Would you have played through?"

"This guy is not a *close* friend, right?" asked Bill.

"Right," I said. "So do you skip the sixteenth?"

"He's lying *on the green?*" asked Bill, considering how he might play through a situation like that.

"Yes," I said.

"I guess I'd have to skip the hole," he said.

And even though it was a hypothetical hole, there was real pain in his voice.

Thus far in this chapter on Guys in Action I've focused on the actions of guys other than myself. Modesty has prevented me from noting that I, too, have demonstrated great decisiveness and courage on several occasions, including a hurricane. And I am not referring here to a previously videotaped hurricane such as Wally saved Lynne from. I am referring to an actual hurricane, named Andrew, which whomped South Florida in 1992 (perhaps you heard about it).

As soon as it was clear that Andrew was headed our way, hordes of people raced to the supermarket to stand in line for hours trying to buy emergency supplies, such as bleach. I have no idea why bleach is such a vital thing to have; all I know is, every time there's a hurricane threat, the helpful radio announcers, who are probably getting huge kickbacks from the bleach industry, urge everybody to get some, and it sells like crazy. In the mounting panic of a prehurricane situation, you find yourself blindly doing whatever the radio announcers tell you. They could tell you that your emergency hurricane supplies should include a dozen long-stemmed red roses, and within minutes you'd be part of the crazed mob at the florist's, climbing over the bodies of weaker consumers.

Anyway, the helpful radio announcers also stressed that it was vital to clear the yard of "all debris and loose objects." That was pretty comical advice, since all a yard *is*, basically, is debris and loose objects. In fact, a good definition of the whole *universe* would be, "a collection of debris and loose objects." Not that this would cut any ice with the helpful radio announcers. They were *adamant* about loose objects. They were saying helpful things like: *"A single grass clipping, propelled by hurricane-force winds, can become a deadly missile that will penetrate your skull and slice your brain into coleslaw."*[6]

With this helpful information echoing in my mind, I spent the morning rushing around gathering yard debris and putting it in the garage, to insure that, once the storm was over, there would be a nice stockpile of

[6]Unless you're a member of Mountain Men Anonymous.

undamaged debris on hand. Then I got to worrying about plywood.

"You *must* get *plywood*," the helpful radio announcers stressed. "It is *absolutely essential that you have plywood* and there is *none available—hahahahahahaha.*"

They were right. I drove around to lumber stores, and they were all sold out. I saw a lot of guys who *had* found plywood; they were driving past me, with sheets of it tied on top of their cars. When I got home, I saw that guys in my own neighborhood had plywood. And I had *nothing*. It was terrible. It was the worst plywood envy I ever had in my life. I wanted plywood so bad I could *taste* it.[7]

And then I thought to myself: Suppose I got some plywood: What the hell would I *do* with it? I have no idea how to attach plywood to a house. Every house I have ever lived in was already assembled when I moved in. I would probably have just leaned my plywood up against the outside walls. (Actually, as Andrew proved, many South Florida homes were constructed via this very economical technique.)

So as darkness came and the wind started picking up, we left our unplywooded house and went to spend the night in the home of some neighbors, Steele and Bobette Reeder. Steele had some plywood, which he

[7]It tasted like chicken.

had nailed over the windows of their master bedroom, thus forming a snug, airtight environment for several families. Tragically, it also formed a snug, airtight environment for the Reeders' dog, Prince.

Here is a tip for anybody who owns a dog and is planning to go through a hurricane in a confined space: *Leave the dog outside.* I don't care if this dog has saved your life on several occasions: You will *not* want to be in the same room with it, because apparently the extreme low barometric pressure associated with a hurricane causes some kind of major disturbance to occur in the dog's digestive system, thereby vastly increasing its output. Even in the best of circumstances, dogs tend to be flatulent, but during Hurricane Andrew, Prince became the Chernobyl Runaway Nuclear Reactor of Farts. There was a visible dog-fart haze in the room. We seriously considered removing some plywood and opening a window, even though the wind was blowing at 160 miles per hour.

But then we had bigger issues to worry about, such as whether the Reeders' house was going to remain standing, which at times we sincerely doubted. People have since asked me: What's it like to be in a hurricane? The answer—and here I will draw upon all my skill and power as a professional wordsmith to enable you to experience, as if firsthand, what this experience feels like—is that it is no fun. There were children there, and they were crying, and the wind was roaring, and Prince was farting, and trees were crashing down outside, and large items were hurtling through the air, and the house was creaking and vibrating and thrashing and groaning as though it was trying to give birth to another house of approximately the same size and weight.

There were three guys in that bedroom—Steele, another neighbor named Olin McKenzie III, and I—and all eyes were upon us, and these eyes were clearly saying: *Is everything going to be okay?*

And so we did what guys do in a situation like this: We decided to Take a Look.

Taking a look is basic guy behavior, as basic as refusing to ask directions. When a car breaks down, for example, most women will generally accept the fact that they know nothing about modern automobile engines, so rather than waste time looking at it, they'll take it to a mechanic. Not a guy. A guy will want to open that hood up and frown at that engine in a thoughtful manner, as though he has some remote clue as to what he is seeing, which he does not. I do this myself. I have no idea what to look for when I lift the hood. Maybe I'm hoping that there will be something really obvious, such as a squid clinging to the manifold.

"Here's the problem right here," I could then say. "There's a squid on the manifold."

But it's never obvious to me. I don't even know which one the "manifold" is. This does not, however, stop me from taking a look. I have taken looks at plumbing problems, electrical problems, construction problems, and computer problems that are light-years beyond my comprehension. If alien beings were forced to land in my driveway because they were having problems with the neutron vector transmaterialization module on their warp drive, I would stride over and take a look.

"Maybe it's flooded," I would suggest, to let the aliens know the caliber of guy they were dealing with.

All guys do this. Ask yourself: What's the first thing the president of the United States does when there's a natural disaster such as a flood? He hops into a helicopter, forms a frowny face, and takes a look at the affected area. Why? What does he expect to accomplish up there? Does he expect to notice something that everybody else missed? ("Hey look! There's a whole bunch of water!")

But the president is a guy—especially our current president—and he has to take a look, and it is for the same reason that Steele, Olin, and I, with the anxious eyes of women and children and Prince the multiple-farting dog upon us, knew that we had to go take a look at the hurricane. We went out the bedroom door, closing it quickly behind us, and stood in the hall. The wind was shrieking out there, and the scary house sounds were much louder, and we could see why: A section of the front wall had become disconnected from the roof, and was bulging and leaning in, as though a giant hand were pushing it.

We guys took a look at this. Then we looked at each other and said, pretty much simultaneously, "Oh, shit." Then we propped a bunch of stuff against the front door and the wall. We did this very nervously, because the wall kept groaning and bulging as though it were about to burst in and convert whoever was standing in front of it into Instant Human Lasagna. We'd skitter over and prop, say, a ladder against it, then we'd skitter away. We also—this is true—stuck a pair of skis there.

> HURRICANE PREPAREDNESS TIP
> Always keep a pair of skis where you can
> get to them quickly in case of emergency.

Then we darted back into the bedroom and closed the door and looked as relaxed as possible considering that the only reason we hadn't peed our pants was that we were too scared.

"It's okay!" we announced. "Nothing to worry about!" Guys in control of a situation.

Then we made eye contact with each other in such a manner as to convey the following information: *Oh, shit.*

But everything worked out. The Reeders' house did not fall down. (I credit the skis.) In the morning, when the wind finally eased up, I made my way back through the downed trees and power lines to my own house, which had pretty much disappeared under a mound of new debris and loose objects. Looking back on it, I realize that this would have been a good time to drink the bleach.

My point is that guys are not merely shallow, childish, irresponsible, unreliable, slovenly, sports-crazed, sex-obsessed, crotch-scratching boors. They *are* all these things, but they are not *merely* these things. As we've seen in this chapter, guys are also capable of achievements that a nonguy cannot even imagine without the aid of strong prescription drugs. So if you're a woman, and you find yourself getting irritated at the guy in your life because he has a few petty guy foibles such as a tendency to blow his nose on the curtains, remember that, if some kind of crisis were to arise, this very same so-called "worthless" guy is fully capable of sizing up the situation in a calm and cool-headed manner, and then—without regard for his own personal safety—going out for a beer. If I were you, I'd encourage him.

# Conclusion

## The Aging Guy:
## Settling Down and Hurling Buicks

*–PLUS–*

## Future Guys of Tomorrow:
## Is There Hope for Humanity?
*(No.)*

WHAT HAPPENS when guys get older? Do they finally realize that there's more to life than clicking the remote control and talking about sports? Do they get in touch with their inner feelings? Do they become mature and wise?

Don't be an idiot. Real guys do not mature, except in the sense of developing longer nose hair. Emotionally, they remain guys. They still do guy stuff; the main difference is that, as they get older and earn more money and find themselves in positions of authority, they can do *bigger* guy stuff. They don't have to settle for merely dropping the occasional commode off of the occasional rooftop to see what happens; they can have *working Air Force bombers.*

Speaking of which, a fine example of an aging guy retaining his essential guyness is George Bush. You may not have agreed with everything he said when he was president,[1] but he was definitely a guy. He'd go up to his compound in Kenneth E. Bunkport IV, Maine, accompanied by the entire massive presidential entourage—aides, advisers, media experts, personal staff, dozens of press people, the Secret Service, the Coast Guard, squadrons of frogpersons, fleets of helicopters, and several submersibles—just so he could drive around real fast in his motorboat. You'd see him on the TV news, zooming across the water, the president of the United States, with an expression *identical* to that of a three-year-old boy pushing a little metal Tonka truck and making a motor sound with his lips, the way little boys instinctively do, like this: *BRRRRMMMMM.*

Looking at him, you knew for a fact that he was not thinking about the unemployment rate, or the status of his proposed federal budget, or problems in the Middle East. You knew *exactly* what he was thinking, because it was the same thing that every guy is thinking when he is driving a motorized vehicle really fast. George

[1] This is partly because he never once publicly completed a sentence.

Bush, the Most Powerful Man in the Most Powerful Nation on Earth, the Leader of the Free World, was thinking: *BRRRRMMMMM.*

Of course not all older guys express their guyness by driving fast. Some of them hurl large objects long distances. I am thinking here of two guys in Texas, an artist/engineer named Richard Clifford and a dentist named John Quincy. One evening, while drinking beer,[2] they got to talking—as guys do when they are opening up and sharing their innermost feelings—about medieval war weapons. Specifically, they got to talking about trebuchets, which are like catapults, but more powerful. Medieval armies used trebuchets to hurl heavy objects, such as boulders, at enemy cities. Sometimes the armies would even throw dead horses. As you can imagine, this was a real morale-breaker:

MEDIEVAL HUSBAND: Hi honey! I'm home from my medieval job in the field of crossbow sales! What's for dinner?

MEDIEVAL WIFE: Your favorite! A nice big mutton . . .

## WHAM

(*A DEAD HORSE COMES CRASHING THROUGH THE CEILING, SPEWING RANCID, MAGGOT-RIDDEN FLESH EVERYWHERE.*)

MEDIEVAL HUSBAND: Actually, I'm not hungry.

MEDIEVAL WIFE: I cannot *wait* for the Renaissance.

• • •

[2]As if I need to tell you this.

So Richard Clifford and John Quincy, being guys, naturally decided that they needed to build a trebuchet. And not just any trebuchet, either. Their goal is to build *the biggest trebuchet in the history of the world*. They want to build a trebuchet that can hurl a Buick two hundred yards—a feat that your medieval armies never even dreamed of.[3]

Clifford and Quincy are serious about this. They have traveled to England to consult with a leading trebuchet expert. They have built and experimented extensively with a small prototype trebuchet, which they use to hurl bowling balls. Quincy has even purchased an eighty-acre property next to his house, *just so the Buick will have a place to land.*

You might think that these are just a couple of isolated eccentrics, but you would be wrong. There are plenty of guys like them. When I wrote a newspaper column about their trebuchet project, I got mail from all over the country. None of this mail was from women. All of it was from adult guys, writing detailed, serious letters expressing *strong* interest in either (a) seeing the Buick get hurled, or (b) building trebuchets of their own. There was no hint, in these letters, that any of these guys thought this was an unusual thing to want to do; it seemed perfectly natural to them to want

[3]The most your medieval armies dreamed of hurling was a Fiat.

to build devices that can hurl heavy objects long distances for no conceivable useful purpose.

Why? Because *this is what guys do.* Guys, no matter how old they get, like to hurl stuff and shoot stuff and go fast and blow stuff up and knock stuff down. This is why, as I pointed out in the introduction to this book, we have a space program. No matter what NASA would have us believe, the purpose of the space program is *not* to benefit the human race by advancing the frontiers of human knowledge. We humans do not need to leave Earth to get to go to a hostile, deadly, alien environment; we already have Miami.

No, the purpose of the space program is to give guys at NASA an excuse to build a whole lot of cool technical stuff and giant rockets that go

BRRRRRRRMMMMMMMMMMMM
*MMMMMMMMMMMMM*

and hurl large objects great distances. If the NASA guys thought that the taxpayers would let them get away with it, they'd try to hit the Moon with a Buick.

True guys continue to be guys, no matter how old or allegedly responsible they get. If you doubt this, go to any sporting event. I am writing these words the morning after attending a National Basketball Association play-off game in Miami between the Miami Heat and the Atlanta Toad Excrements (not that I am biased). The crowd around me was mostly guys in their forties and older—husbands and fathers with responsible, demanding South Florida jobs such as stockbroker, doctor, lawyer, narcotics kingperson, etc. I am certain that these guys think of themselves as mature and rational individuals. I'm also certain that they believe they are, as males, more logical than females, and less likely to be governed by their feelings. They would tell you that, quite frankly, they are a little embarrassed by the way their wives tend to cry during the sad part of a romantic movie. Because after all, it's just a *movie;* there's no reason to get all *emotional* about it.

That's what these guys would tell you, if you asked them. But you should not ask them during a play-off basketball game, because they are very busy reacting rationally and logically to events on the court.

"YOU SUCK, SEIKALY!" they are informing Miami Heat center Rony Seikaly. "YOU *SUCK!*" they add, by way of clarification. Seikaly has just missed two free throws with less than two minutes to go, and the middle-aged guys all hate him. They are on their feet, their bodies vibrating with fury, their faces dark red and contorted with rage, the muscle cords standing out in their necks. They have never, ever, hated anybody, including Hitler, as much as they hate Rony Seikaly at this particular moment. Hitler was a bad person, yes, but he did not miss important free throws in the playoffs.

These men want to *kill* Rony Seikaly. They want to see him dismembered and have his eyeballs eaten by rats right there on the basketball court. They want him to ...

Wait a minute! Rony has grabbed an offensive rebound! He's putting the ball back up! It's going to go . . . YES! SCORE! WAY TO GO, RONY! YES! HIGH FIVE! MY MAN RONY!! The middle-aged guys *love* Rony Seikaly. They want to kiss him on the lips. They want to fly to a medical clinic in Sweden and undergo major elective surgery so they can have Rony's children. They cannot believe they are so fortunate as to be on the same *planet* as such a magnificent human being as Rony Seikaly. He is a *giant*. He is a *god*. He is . . .

He is *not guarding his man*! His man is blowing right past him for an easy layup! Shit! YOU SUCK, SEIKALY! YOU *SUCK*!! YOU . . .

You see my point. Guys, even as they get older, remain deeply concerned about the basic guy issues, as discussed extensively in this book and summarized in the following chart.

| Issues That Are of Major Concern to Guys | Issues That Are Not of Major Concern to Guys |
| --- | --- |
| The play-offs | Global warming, unless it affects the play-offs |
| Whether they are being tailgated | Whether they are tailgating |
| Who won the 1962 World Series | What happens to laundry after you drop it on the floor |
| Eating | Cooking |
| Sex | The specific person they are having sex with |

These are the core values that have been preserved by guys throughout the millennia. But what about the future? What will happen when the current generation of guys passes away, possibly as a result of trebuchet-related injuries? Is the next generation ready to step up and carry on the guy tradition, with all the responsibilities it entails? This is the question that prompted me to initiate a probing, heart-to-heart conversation with my son.

"Robert," I said. "I need to talk to you about a matter of some importance to the future of humanity."

"Not now," he said. "Me and Trey are setting golf balls on fire."

So the future of guyness looks bright. If you need further proof, consider the following anecdote told to me by a friend of mine, Kathi Goldmark. She had spent a couple of days at a Miami hotel, and one employee had been so helpful that Kathi, when she got home, decided to send a letter of praise to the employee's boss. She finished the letter, but did not remove it from the typewriter until the next morning, when, in a hurry, she took it out, signed it, and began to fold it to put it into the envelope. This was when she happened to notice that, at the bottom of this nice, polite letter she was about to send to a hotel executive she had never met, her nine-year-old son, Tony, had neatly typed:

p.s. Don't forget to fart.

This incident causes me to experience conflicting emotions. On the one hand, I feel a tremendous sense of sorrow and loss caused by the fact that Kathi did not actually send the letter. But at the same time I feel great happiness, knowing that young guys like Tony will be coming along to fill the void that will exist some day when we older guys finally move on to that Big Keg Party in the Sky.

Because let's face it, the human race needs guys. I realize that sometimes we can be annoying to you non-guys, but just try to imagine what the world would be like without us. Okay, granted, it would smell better. Also there would be a dramatic reduction in violence, intolerance, and public nose-picking. But these negatives are far outweighed by the numerous contributions that guys make to society—positive contributions, vital contributions, contributions that are in no way diminished by the fact that I can't, offhand, think of what they are.

No matter. Guys, and guyness, are here to stay. And although the tone of this book has been somewhat flippant, I want to close by saying, in all sincerity, that I hope the effort I have made in these pages will in some small way improve the level of understanding between guys and persons of other genders, so that some day this fragile and troubled world in which we all must exist together will truly be a better and more caring place in which to blah blah blah p.s. Don't forget to fart.

# Index

ABOUT THE TYPE

This book was set in Photina, a typeface designed by José Mendoza in 1971. It is a very elegant design with high legibility and its close character fit has made it a popular choice for use in quality magazines and art gallery publications.